WERBEL'S

Health Insurance

(Sickness & Accident)

PRIMER

A training manual for prospective
Health Insurance Agents

Edited by
BERNARD G. WERBEL

Werbel
PUBLISHING CO., INC.
595 Old Willets Path, Smithtown, L. I., N. Y. 11787
Phones: In N. Y. C., (212) 261-6222 • In L. I., (516) 234-1114

SEVENTH EDITION, FIRST PRINTING
Copyright © Werbel Publishing Co., Inc. 1976
595 Old Willets Path, Smithtown, L. I., New York 11787

•

Copyright © 1957, 1961, 1963, 1966, 1969, 1972, and 1976
by Bernard G. Werbel and Werbel Publishing Co., Inc.

•

All rights reserved. This book, or parts thereof, may not be reproduced by magnetic tape, phonograph records, or in any form whatsoever, without written permission from the publisher.

Printed in the United States of America

FOREWORD

This primer is designed to give a prospective Health Insurance Agent (or Broker) a fundamental knowledge of this comprehensive subject, and to aid him in his preparation for State Licensing Examinations. The text material is based upon the accepted practices and policies of the industry as well as the laws, regulations, and procedures applicable in most States. It has been scrutinized carefully (for factual accuracy) by experts in the Education and Training Departments of several insurance companies which specialize in the issuance of this type of coverage.

The subject matter is presented in Question and Answer style. This format generates greater participation by the reader and enables him to retain the information for a longer period of time.

Many of the questions contain subject matter which is comparable to that which has appeared in State examinations, including queries that are based on the latest changes in the Health Insurance industry.

Furthermore, the Self-Quiz appearing at the end of this publication enables the student to verify the accuracy of his understanding of the subject.

This primer has been used successfully throughout the country by numerous educational institutions conducting regular courses for prospective Health Insurance Licensees as well as by Managers and General Agents in their own training programs.

Although the purpose of this primer is to aid prospective licensees, many persons who have been selling Health Insurance for some time find it stimulating to refresh their knowledge of the basic facts contained herein.

Bernard G. Werbel
Editor

Smithtown, N. Y. 11787
September 1978

TABLE OF CONTENTS

Health Insurance	1
Health Policies	3
Miscellaneous Provisions	27
Required Uniform Policy Provisions	33
Optional Uniform Policy Provisions	37
Other Requirements of the Law	41
Underwriting	43
Classes of Policies	51
Major Medical Insurance	57
Group Insurance	65
Blue Cross and Blue Shield	71
Group Practice Plans	72
Medicare	73
Insurance Law	79
Review Questions	93
Glossary of Health Insurance Terms	107
Self-Quiz	123

HEALTH INSURANCE

Question 1:
What is a Health Insurance Policy, and what is its purpose?
Answer:
A Health Insurance Policy is a contract between an insurer (an insurance company or an association authorized to issue such contracts) and an Insured (an individual or group of individuals) in which the insurer agrees to the payment of certain Benefits to the Insured or his Beneficiary for specified losses sustained by the Insured, resulting from sickness or accident.

Unlike many other types of insurance policies, a new policy is not issued every year or every three years. The original policy remains in force until terminated (either by the Insured or the insurance company). Many policies remain in force for 10, 20, or even 30 years and if changes are necessary they are made by endorsement.

Agents (and Brokers) should keep this in mind when reviewing a client's policies. The coverage under an old policy may be broader or more limited than new policies currently being issued.

Question 2:
Against what losses does Health Insurance provide protection?
Answer:
Health Insurance Policies can be separated into two main categories; those affording Benefits for loss of income due to accident or sickness (known as Disability Income Policies) and those affording reimbursement for medical, surgical, and hospital expenses due to accident or sickness (commonly referred to as Hospitalization Policies).

Question 3:
Do all Health Policies afford coverage for both loss of income and reimbursement for medical expenses in one policy?
Answer:
Not necessarily, various combinations of coverage are available. For example, protection may be afforded for:

a. Loss of income resulting from accidents only, or resulting from accidents and/or sicknesses.

b. Reimbursement for medical expenses and loss of income resulting from accidents only, or resulting from accidents and/or sicknesses.

c. Reimbursement for medical expenses resulting from accidents only, or resulting from accidents and/or sicknesses without affording coverage for loss of income.

NOTE: Usually, coverage for loss resulting from sicknesses only is not issued as a separate policy.

Question 4:
How are Benefits paid?
Answer:
There are three methods of payment:

a. Income payments — a specified sum payable monthly or weekly (Income Benefit).

HEALTH INSURANCE

b. Lump sum payments which are specified in the policy (Lump Sum Benefit).

c. Reimbursement for specified expenses (Medical Expense Benefit).

Question 5:
Why is a Health Policy an important form of coverage?
Answer:
Frequently, an illness (or an accident) results in the incurring of prohibitive medical, surgical, and hospital expenses. A Health Insurance Policy can afford coverage for these expenses and provide disability income as well. This is particularly important with reference to the breadwinner of a family.

In 1974, the average per capita expenditure on personal health care was $485. According to information compiled by the Health Insurance Institute, eight out of ten civilians in the United States were protected by some form of *private* Health Insurance in 1975. This represented 172 million Americans. Insurance companies cover 47% of the American civilians with some form of *private* Health Insurance.

Question 6:
How does a sickness or an accident affect the average family?
Answer:
The earned income of the breadwinner is the foundation of the family's economy. If his earned income is discontinued as a result of a sickness or an accident, a financial crisis may result. The high cost of medical treatment may bankrupt the average family. A comprehensive Health Insurance Program (Disability Income Coverage and Medical Expense Coverage) should be arranged to avoid this type of catastrophe.

It is the duty of the Agent (or Broker) to explain that this tremendous loss possibility is insurable, and should be covered.

Question 7:
How does a comprehensive Health Insurance Program benefit the community?
Answer:
If a financial crisis of this nature arises, after an uninsured (or underinsured) family has exhausted its savings, the family must seek assistance from relatives, friends, or the community. A Health Insurance Program eliminates the need for this type of public or private assistance.

Question 8:
Who are prospects for Health Insurance?
Answer:
Everyone who has an earned income or who may require medical attention at some future time is a prospect. There are very few persons who are not prospects.

Even though persons aged 65 and over are covered by Medicare (Basic and Supplementary Coverage), they should consider the advisability of carrying supplemental protection in an insurance company.

HEALTH POLICIES

There are many forms of Health Policies. Unlike other lines of insurance, there is no rigid standardization of forms. The Health Insurance Association of America (750 Third Avenue, New York, New York 10017) gathers statistics and facts pertaining to the underwriting of Health Insurance. However, each insurance company drafts and files (for approval) its own policies, forms, and premium rates with the Insurance Department in each State in which it writes insurance. It is only after such approval has been obtained that policies may be sold in the State involved.

The value of any Health Insurance Policy is determined by the clauses and the interpretation thereof. In order to enable a prospective Insured to properly evaluate a Health Policy, a clear explanation must be rendered with respect to the favorable or unfavorable phraseology of a policy pertaining to the Benefits afforded thereunder and the definitions and restrictions contained therein.

The following questions deal with virtually all of the coverages available in Health Policies, including Individual and Group Hospitalization and Major Medical as well as Disability Income Protection (Salary Continuation) Policies.

Question 1:
What are some of the provisions contained in a Health Policy?

Answer:
The policy is made up of various sections, e.g., the Insuring Agreement, Consideration Clause, Policy Term, Schedule of Benefits, Benefits Provisions, Exclusions, Miscellaneous Provisions, Required Provisions, and Optional Provisions.

Question 2:
What is the Insuring Agreement?

Answer:
An Insuring Agreement defines the conditions under which Benefits will be paid (subject to the exclusions and limitations of the policy).

The following is an example of an Insuring Agreement of a Disability Income Policy:

"The insurance company hereby insures the person named in Statement 1 of the copy of the application for this policy attached hereto (herein called the Insured) and subject to the limitations, exceptions, and provisions of this policy, promises to pay indemnity for loss covered by this policy resulting from injury or sickness to the extent herein provided.

"Injury, wherever used in this policy, means accidental bodily injury caused by an accident occurring while this policy is in force and resulting directly and independently of all other causes in loss covered by this policy.

HEALTH POLICIES

"Sickness, wherever used in this policy, means sickness contracted and commencing after this policy has been in force not less than 14 days after its effective date and resulting in loss covered by this policy."

NOTE: Some policies specify 30 days (instead of 14 days); and some policies do not contain a Probationary Period.

Question 3:
Is the above clause a Standard Insuring Agreement?

Answer:
No, it is a good example of an Insuring Agreement. However, all insurance companies do not use the same wording. Furthermore, if a policy covers accident losses only, the sickness portion is omitted.

Question 4:
What is the chief variation in the Accident Insuring Agreement?

Answer:
The chief variation is the use of the phrase "injury caused by accidental means" instead of "accidental bodily injury".

Question 5:
What is meant by "accidental means" and how does it differ from "accidental bodily injury"?

Answer:
"Accidental means" is defined as an unforeseen, unexpected, unintended cause of an accident. It is more limiting than "accidental bodily injury". It requires an accidental cause, while accidental bodily injury just requires bodily injury. "Accidental means" deals with the cause of the accident. "Accidental bodily injury" deals with the effect of the accident. The following example illustrates the difference:

A man, while moving a sofa, injures his back. Although there is an accidental bodily injury, there is no "accidental means"; i.e., there was no accidental cause. He intended to move the sofa and in doing so caused the back injury. If he had slipped or tripped on a rug or some other object, the accident would have been caused by "accidental means".

Question 6:
Is it very difficult for an insurance company to distinguish between one type of injury and another?

Answer:
Yes. However, today, most insurance companies use the Accidental Bodily Injury Clause. This clause is often referred to as the Accidental Result Clause whereas the other is referred to as the Accidental Means Clause.

Question 7:
Although most insurance companies have stopped using the Accidental Means Clause, what about old policies containing that clause?

HEALTH POLICIES

Answer:

Some insurance companies add endorsements using the more liberal wording or process claims as though the policies contained the more liberal wording.

Question 8:

Are there any other variations in the Accident Insuring Agreement?

Answer:

Yes. Many insurance companies use the phrase "directly and independently of all other causes". Some insurance companies use this phrase only in connection with lifetime Accident Coverage.

Question 9:

What is meant by "directly and independently of all other causes"?

Answer:

The following illustration indicates the meaning of this language. If a man who suffers a heart attack while driving his car, loses control of his car and is injured in the resulting accident, the injuries caused by the accident would probably not be covered under the Accident Insuring Agreement portion of a policy because the heart attack was the cause of the accident. The accident was not caused directly and independently of all other causes.

Question 10:

Does this create a problem in handling claims?

Answer:

No. Usually, medical evidence makes it possible to determine whether or not the impaired health of the person was a major cause of the accident.

Question 11:

Are there differences in the wording of the Sickness Insuring Clause?

Answer:

The chief differences are:

a. The sickness or disease must commence or be contracted while the policy is in force.

b. Coverage is afforded if the sickness first manifests itself during the policy period even though it may have been contracted prior to the inception date of the policy.

c. The policy may specify a Probationary Period, and if so, it may be 14 days, 30 days, or some other specified period of time.

Question 12:

What is a Probationary Period?

Answer:

A Probationary Period is a specified number of days after the date of the issuance of the policy, during which coverage is not afforded for sickness. Sometimes, it is referred to as the "Incubation Period".

HEALTH POLICIES

Question 13:
What purpose does the Probationary Period limitation serve?

Answer:
This limitation is designed to eliminate Benefits for a sickness actually contracted before the policy went into effect. It states that the policy will cover only those sicknesses which the Insured contracts after the Probationary Period.

Question 14:
What happens if the Insured contracts a sickness during the Probationary Period?

Answer:
He is not eligible for Benefits for that disability regardless of its duration.

Question 15:
Disability Income Policies also contain an Elimination Period (Waiting Period). How does it differ from a Probationary Period?

Answer:
An Elimination Period is the period of time between the date a disability commenced and the date the Benefits are payable. Benefits are not payable for the Elimination Period. Generally, protection is afforded on the basis of one of the following Elimination Periods: 7, 14, 30, 60, 90, 180, or 365 days.

A Probationary Period is only effective for a limited number of days after a policy has been issued. Once the specified number of days has elapsed, the Probationary Period is no longer applicable. Whereas, an Elimination Period is applicable every time the Insured is disabled (as defined in the policy).

Question 16:
What is the Consideration Clause?

Answer:
All contracts, to be legal, must contain an offer, an acceptance, and a consideration. In a Health Policy, the consideration consists of the Insured's statements made in the application (a copy of which is attached to and becomes a part of the policy) and the payment of the Premium.

Question 17:
What is the Policy Term?

Answer:
The Policy Term (stated in the Consideration Clause) is the period for which the policy is intended to run. Usually, it is stated in terms of the type of Premium payable, e.g., Annual Premium for one year; Monthly Premium for one month, etc.

HEALTH POLICIES

Question 18:
How long is the Policy Term, and when does it begin and end?

Answer:
The Policy Term may be annual, semiannual, quarterly, monthly, or weekly. Generally, it begins and ends at 12 o'clock Noon Standard Time at the residence of the Insured.

Question 19:
What is the Schedule of Benefits?

Answer:
The Schedule of Benefits is the section of a policy which lists the maximum amounts payable for the respective coverages for which protection is afforded.

Question 20:
What are the Benefit Provisions?

Answer:
A series of sections each of which pertains to a specific Benefit, e.g., Disability Income Benefit (Total Disability, confining and nonconfining, and Partial Disability), Accidental Death, Dismemberment, and Loss of Sight Benefit, Elective Indemnities, Double Indemnities, Physicians' Expense for Nondisabling Injury, Medical Expense, Hospital Expense Benefit (room, board, and extra charges), Surgical Expense Benefit, Physicians' Expense Benefit, Nurses' Expense Benefit, Maternity Benefit, etc. Some Disability Income Policies also include Benefits for loss of speech or hearing. Note: Not all of these Benefits are contained in every policy.

Question 21:
How is Total Disability defined in an Accident Insuring Agreement of a Disability Income Policy?

Answer:
There are many variations in the definition of Total Disability, primarily in the interpretation of the Insured's inability to work, as follows:

a. Some insurance companies define Total Disability as "complete inability to engage in work pertaining to his occupation or profession".

b. Other insurance companies use the following definition of Total Disability: "complete inability to engage in any gainful occupation for which he is reasonably fitted". However, for the first 24 months of his disability, the Insured is deemed to be Totally Disabled if he is unable to perform any and every duty of his occupation and is not engaged in any gainful occupation. This definition, which is referred to as "24 months — His Occupation" includes a limiting provision which is worded as follows: "not engaged in *any* gainful occupation". This limitation means that although the Insured is wholly unable to work at his occupation, he does not qualify as being Totally Disabled if he is gainfully employed in any other occupation.

HEALTH POLICIES

c. According to the policies issued by some insurance companies, Total Disability means complete inability of the Insured to engage in his occupation. However, after a specified period of continuous disability (e.g., 52 weeks, 24 months, 60 months, 7 years, 10 years, to age 55, or to age 65), the definition of Total Disability is modified to mean "complete inability of the Insured to engage in any gainful occupation for which he is reasonably fitted by education, training, or experience". Some insurance companies also include "with due consideration of his prior economic status".

NOTE 1: This is an example of a Primary and a Secondary definition of Total Disability.

NOTE 2: In policies affording long-term coverage for continuous disability, some insurance companies use the following wording: "inability to engage in the policyholder's regular occupation".

d. Some insurers use the following: "Total Disability means complete inability of the Insured to engage in any gainful occupation".

Question 22:
What is an Accidental Bodily Injury Time Limit Clause?

Answer:
The policies of some insurance companies do not have a time limit, i.e., the definition merely states that Total Disability resulting from an accident must commence while the policy is in force.

The policies of some insurance companies contain a specified time limit, e.g., Total Disability must commence within 30, 60, or 90 days after the date of the accident. In many cases, a disability due to an accident does not manifest itself immediately (or even within a short time) after the accident. The longer the interval between an accident and the commencement of Total Disability, the greater the difficulty in establishing the causal relationship between the two. For example, if a policy has a 60-day clause and the Insured did not become disabled until 80 days after an accident, he would not be entitled to collect any Benefits under the Accident Insuring Clause. However, if the policy contained a Sickness Total Disability Benefit, the Insured might be eligible to receive Benefits in accordance with the Sickness Insuring Agreement.

Question 23:
If an Insured became Totally Disabled due to an accident, how long would he be entitled to collect Benefits?

Answer:
If the Insured remains Totally Disabled beyond the Elimination Period (if any), a Weekly or Monthly Indemnity would be paid for the Benefit Period specified in the schedule and according to the definition of Total Disability in the policy (e.g., 52 weeks, 24 months, 60 months, 7 years, 10 years, to age 55, 65, or for the lifetime of the Insured).

HEALTH POLICIES

Question 24:

Do all policies limit disability income payments to a specified period of time if the Insured is prevented continuously from performing every duty pertaining to his occupation?

Answer:

No, many insurance companies afford lifetime Accident Coverage. A few insurance companies write lifetime Sickness Coverage; however, the Total Disability must commence before a specified age (e.g., 45, 50, or 55) and must be continuous. If the Total Disability begins after the specified age, coverage is afforded for five years or up to age 65. Most insurance companies require that the Insured be unable to perform the duties of *his occupation* for an initial period, e.g., 2, 5, or 10 years.

NOTE: All insurance companies require the Insured to be under the regular care and attention of a licensed physician other than himself.

Question 25:

How frequently must the Insured be examined by his physician?

Answer:

The nature of the disability and the treatment necessary for the particular individual involved determines the frequency with which examinations must be performed by the Insured's physician. If the condition of the Insured unquestionably does not require the services of a doctor on a regular basis, the Insured would be absolved of compliance with this requirement. For example, a person who is blind as a result of an accident need not be examined by a doctor regularly to prove that he is disabled. However, the insurance company reserves the right to examine the claimant at any reasonable time.

Question 26:

Do insurers use other sources of information (not medical) to determine whether or not an Insured is Totally (or Partially) Disabled?

Answer:

Yes. Many insurance companies utilize the services of credit reporting firms to ascertain whether or not an Insured (who claims to be Totally Disabled) is working. Furthermore, if an Insured has stated that he is Partially Disabled, these sources of information are also used to determine the extent to which the Insured is working, and whether or not he is unable to perform one or more of the important daily duties pertaining to his occupation.

Question 27:

What is Partial Disability and what is the Partial Disability Benefit under a Disability Income Policy?

Answer:

The definition of Partial Disability varies. Usually, if the Insured is unable to perform one or more (but not all) of the important duties of his occupation, and is under the regular care and attention of a legally qualified physician (other than himself), he is considered to be Partially Disabled. Usually, the Partial Disability Benefit is 50% of the Total

HEALTH POLICIES

Disability Benefit and is generally payable for up to a maximum of six months.

Some insurers offer a Partial Disability Rehabilitation Provision. To be eligible for Benefits thereunder, the Insured must be either: (a) unable to engage in his occupation for more than one-half of the time usually required for full-time performance of the duties of his occupation; (b) participating in a government sponsored or other professionally planned vocational rehabilitation program approved by the insurer.

NOTE 1: Some Disability Income Policies do not afford protection for Partial Disability; however, some insurance companies offer this coverage for an additional Premium (by endorsement).

NOTE 2: Some insurers utilize a Residual Disability Clause which states that if the Insured returns to his regular occupation and his income is reduced because he is disabled (e.g., by 25%, but less than 75%), the insurer will pay a reduced Benefit (computed either based upon a fomula or a stipulated percentage) for as long as the Insured's income is reduced because of his disability. There are a number of variations of this Residual Disability Benefit. Most insurers do not afford both Benefits concurrently. Since many different formulas and percentages are used, a Producer should be prepared to make a full and complete comparison.

Question 28:
If the Insured were able to work part of the time, would he be entitled to collect for a Partial Disability?
Answer:
Yes. If an Insured were able to work for a few hours a day or if he were able to work during his regular hours, but unable to perform one or more of the important duties of his occupation (salesman making outside calls, lawyer going to court, etc.); generally, he would be considered Partially Disabled.

Question 29:
Must Partial Disability follow Total Disability (resulting from accident or sickness)?
Answer:
Most insurance companies specify that Partial Disability caused by an accident must immediately follow Total Disability caused by accidental bodily injury for which reimbursement is payable under the policy. However, some insurance companies pay for Partial Disability caused by accidental bodily injury even though it does not immediately follow Total Disability.

With respect to disability resulting from *sickness,* Partial Disability caused by sickness must immediately follow Total Disability caused by sickness for which reimbursement is payable under the policy.

Question 30:
Do all policies have a Sickness Benefit?
Answer:
No. Many policies cover only the accident hazard.

HEALTH POLICIES

Question 31:
Are policies written to cover only sickness?

Answer:
No, unless the applicant has an Accident Disability Policy in force with the same insurance company. The Sickness Benefit Period may be less than or equal to (but never longer than) the Benefit Period for the Accident Policy.

Question 32:
Is the Sickness Coverage issued as a separate policy?

Answer:
No. Usually, it is a Benefit in a policy which also covers indemnities for accidental injury.

Question 33:
Is the Sickness Benefit the same as the Accident Benefit?

Answer:
No. The Sickness Benefit is limited to income payments for Total Disability and medical expenses. There is no Sickness Benefit for Dismemberment, Death, Elective Indemnities, Physicians' Expense for Non-disabling Injuries, or Double Indemnity Coverage.

NOTE: Dismemberment Provision-Presumptive Disability: Some insurance companies issue Noncancellable Policies which pay full Total Disability Benefits for blindness, double dismemberment, loss of use of two limbs, total loss of speech, loss of hearing in both ears, whether as a result of accident or sickness.

Question 34:
Is the Total Disability Income Benefit for sickness payable under the same conditions as in the case of an accident?

Answer:
The definition of Total Disability for sickness or accident is usually the same, e.g., the Insured is wholly and continuously disabled and prevented from performing each and every duty pertaining to his occupation and under the regular care and attendance of a physician, surgeon, or osteopath. However, some policies contain a Probationary Period for sickness; and some (older policies) contain a Confining Clause for sickness.

For example, under the limitations of one Confining Clause, the Insured must be unable to perform each and every duty pertaining to his occupation; must not receive any earnings for other work or service; must be under the regular care and attendance of a physician; and must be confined within doors. Under such policy, the Monthly Indemnity might be paid for as long as the Insured lives if he is necessarily and continuously confined within doors. Coverage is not terminated if, in accordance with the Insured's doctor's instructions, the Insured travels

HEALTH POLICIES

to or from a hospital or to or from his doctor's office for necessary treatment.

NOTE: Under such a policy, an Insured may collect his Monthly Indemnity for a nonconfining sickness for not more than three consecutive months, provided that it commenced while the policy was in force or immediately followed an Indemnity Period for a confining sickness.

The Disability Income Policies of some insurance companies contain a broader definition of Total Disability, i.e., "complete inability of the Insured to engage in his regular occupation or profession, except that if the period of disability is continuous for 60 months, then during any further continuance of that period of disability for which Monthly Income Benefits may be payable, Total Disability means complete inability of the Insured to engage in any gainful occupation in which the Insured might be expected to be engaged, with due regard to his training, background, and prior economic status".

NOTE: Generally, the phrase "regular occupation or profession" is interpreted to include the Insured's occupation in a broad sense. For instance, surgeons or pediatricians are engaged in the medical profession.

A more liberal definition of Total Disability refers only to the Insured's "inability to engage in the Insured's regular occupation". For example, some insurance companies afford coverage if the Insured is merely unable to work in his own occupational specialty, such as: surgeon, radiologist, pathologist, dermatologist, orthodontist, trial lawyer, patent lawyer, etc.

Question 35:
What is meant by confinement in the home, a hospital, or a sanitarium?
Answer:
The Insured must be disabled by an illness which confines him to his home, a hospital, or a sanitarium. This type of Benefit is known as a House Confining Benefit.

Question 36:
Could an Insured be eligible for any Benefit whatsoever if he were not confined?
Answer:
Most policies containing the House Confining Benefit provide for the payment of some Benefit to the Insured if he is not confined. Coverage is afforded in one of two ways:

a. Reducing the income payments by 50% if he is not confined, or

b. Reducing the maximum period of time for which Benefits will be paid. For example, some insurance companies pay Benefits for 5 years if the Insured is house-confined, but for only one year if he is not house-confined.

HEALTH POLICIES

Question 37:

Is the Sickness Income Benefit as broad as the Accident Income Benefit?

Answer:

Practically all insurance companies issue a policy affording Income Benefit for the lifetime of the Insured for Accident Total Disability.

Some insurance companies issue a policy affording a Lifetime Benefit for Sickness Total Disability. However, a few of these insurance companies require that the Insured must be confined. If not, the Monthly Indemnity is either reduced by a stipulated percentage or the Benefit Period is limited to a shorter period of time.

Some insurance companies issue policies with Lifetime Sickness Benefits. However (generally), in order to receive Lifetime Sickness Benefits under these policies, the sickness must commence prior to a predetermined age, e.g., 45, 50, or 55; and must be continuous. If Total Disability (Sickness) occurs after the stipulated age, the coverage would be limited to a specified period (e.g., 24 months or 60 months).

Many insurance companies issue policies which provide sickness income payments to the Insured until he reaches his 65th birthday. Such policies do not require confinement. However, the Premium for a policy containing a Limit of Liability for sickness to age 65 is much higher and the standards of underwriting for this type of coverage are much stricter with respect to height, weight, age, and condition of health.

NOTE: If the Insured is actively working, many insurance companies will renew the policy to age 72 on a Guaranteed Renewable basis. Generally, Benefits beginning after age 65 are limited to 2 years for Sickness and Accident Coverage.

Question 38:

In which other ways is Sickness Coverage more limited than Accident Coverage?

Answer:

Generally, Accident Coverage is afforded on a world-wide basis, whereas Sickness Coverage is limited to the United States and Canada.

Most insurance companies will issue a travel endorsement if requested to do so. This endorsement extends the policy to cover a specified trip for a limited period of time. The insurance company will grant the extension of coverage (without additional charge) if the Insured does not intend to visit an exceptionally hazardous area (e.g., war area, jungle, or where primitive conditions prevail with respect to sanitation and health facilities). The duration of the trip is also an important underwriting consideration. If the trip is to be extremely long, claim settlements, Premium payments, etc. may become difficult problems.

NOTE: Many insurance companies issue policies which do not contain any travel restrictions.

HEALTH POLICIES

Question 39:
What is the Accidental Death Benefit?

Answer:
The Accidental Death Benefit is the sum that is paid to the Beneficiary in the event of the accidental death of the Insured. This loss payment is called the Principal Sum.

Question 40:
Must death take place at the time of the accident for the Accidental Death Benefit to be payable?

Answer:
No, the Death Benefit (Principal Sum) will be paid if:

a. The Insured suffers continuous Total Disability which commenced within 20 days (or 30 days) from the date of the accident, provided that death occurs within a specified number of weeks from the date of the accident (e.g., 200 weeks or 2 years).

b. Death occurs within 90 days of the date of the accident even though the Insured was not Totally Disabled.

NOTE: In order to create a greater incentive to renew a policy, some insurance companies increase the Principal Sum with each renewal until it reaches 150% of the original amount (e.g., $1,000 Benefit to $1,500). This is called the Accumulation Clause. The Premium is not increased. Thus, the policyholder has an added incentive to renew the coverage in the same insurance company.

Question 41:
What is: (a) a dismemberment and (b) loss of sight?

Answer:
Dismemberment is defined as the severance of limbs at or above the wrists or ankle joints. Loss of sight means complete, total, and irrecoverable loss of sight of one or both eyes.

NOTE: Many insurance companies afford coverage for "loss of use" of limbs and include Benefits for loss of speech and hearing.

Question 42:
What is the Dismemberment and Loss of Sight Benefit?

Answer:
This Benefit is a lump sum payment for the loss of limbs or eyesight based on a printed schedule in the policy.

Most insurance companies use the phrase "Principal Sum" with the Accidental Death Benefit and the phrase "Capital Sum" with the Dismemberment and Loss of Sight Benefit. However, some insurance companies use the term "Principal Sum" for both accidental death, dismemberment, and loss of sight. It is related to the Weekly or Monthly In-

HEALTH POLICIES

come Benefit (e.g., 200 weeks of Benefits or a dollar amount limited to 50 times the Monthly Income, such as $25,000).

NOTE: In subsequent references to accidental death, the lump sum payment will be called the Principal Sum. In references to dismemberment and loss of sight, it will be called the Capital Sum.

Question 43:
In order to qualify for the Dismemberment and Loss of Sight Benefit, must the dismemberment and/or loss of sight occur at the time of the accident?
Answer:
No. Usually, the Capital Sum will be paid if the Insured suffers a dismemberment and/or loss of sight: (a) within 90 days after the accident even though he had not been disabled immediately prior to his injury; or (b) within a continuous period of Total Disability resulting from the injury but not later than two years after the accident and before termination of income payable for the Total Disability. Some insurance companies pay the Capital Sum if Total Disability commences within a specified number of days after the accident (e.g., 30 days) provided that the dismemberment and/or loss of sight is sustained within a stipulated period (e.g., 200 weeks).

Question 44:
If the Insured is disabled for an extended period of time and subsequently dies or suffers a dismemberment and/or loss of sight, does the insurance company subtract the weekly or monthly payments previously made from the payment of the Principal Sum or the Capital Sum?
Answer:
Some insurance companies subtract the payments made previously from the lump sum payment.

Question 45:
Must the Insured accept the Capital Sum payment in the event of a dismemberment and/or loss of sight?
Answer:
If the Insured suffers a single dismemberment or loss of one eye, he must accept the applicable Capital Sum. However, if the Insured suffers a double dismemberment (two limbs) or loss of two eyes, some insurance companies will permit him to apply for periodic income payments instead of compelling him to accept the applicable Capital Sum. He must make the request in writing prior to the payment of the Capital Sum, and the policy must contain a provision for income payments.

NOTE: Some insurance companies pay the Income Benefit as well as the Dismemberment and Loss of Sight Benefit.

Question 46:
How long are these income payments continued?

HEALTH POLICIES

Answer:

For the period of Total Disability or the maximum period of the insurance company's liability as specified in the policy. In any event, the Insured is guaranteed a minimum amount equal to the Capital Sum payment.

Question 47:

If the Insured dies before this minimum amount has been paid, is the balance paid to his estate or Beneficiary?

Answer:

Yes. The balance is paid to a Named Beneficiary, or if a Beneficiary is not named, to the Insured's estate.

However, the policies of some insurance companies provide that if the Insured or the Beneficiary is a minor or legally incompetent; or if a Beneficiary had not been designated, the insurance company will pay Benefits up to $1,000 to a relative of the Insured who apparently is entitled to the money. This clause is known as the Facility of Payment Clause.

Question 48:

If the Insured has received a Capital Sum, and becomes disabled again, is he eligible for additional Benefits?

Answer:

If the policy is renewable at the option of the insurance company, the payment of the Capital Sum usually relieves the insurance company of any liability with respect to any injury sustained subsequent thereto.

However, if the policy does not give the insurance company the right to refuse to renew, the payment of the Capital Sum does not terminate the policy or any of its Benefits.

Question 49:

What is the Elective Indemnities Benefit?

Answer:

If the Insured suffers an accidental bodily injury which results in a dislocation, fracture, or the amputation of fingers or toes, he may elect (within 30 days of the date of the accident) to receive a lump sum payment in accordance with a printed schedule of Elective Indemnities instead of the regular Income Indemnities.

Question 50:

What is the advantage of a lump sum payment in lieu of Income Indemnities?

Answer:

The bodily injury may not disable the Insured, or the disability may be of a very short duration. Under such circumstances, the lump sum payment may be greater than the Income Benefit for which he would

HEALTH POLICIES

be eligible. However, if the injury will disable him for an extended period, the Insured may elect to receive the Income Benefit in lieu of the lump sum payment.

Question 51:
Is the Elective Indemnities Clause the same in all insurance companies?
Answer:
No. Some insurance companies use a clause which guarantees certain sums as minimum indemnities, and if the Insured is continuously disabled for an extended period, he may collect, in addition, the applicable amount in excess of such minimums. This clause is known as Minimum Indemnities for Specified Losses.

Question 52:
What is a Nondisabling Injury Benefit or a Physicians' Expense Benefit for a Nondisabling Injury?
Answer:
If, as a result of an accident, the Insured sustains accidental bodily injury which does not cause Total or Partial Disability but requires treatment by a physician, the insurance company will reimburse the Insured for such treatment up to a Maximum Benefit equal to one week's indemnity, or one-fourth of the monthly indemnity if the Income Benefit is payable monthly. This Benefit is not payable if any other Benefits are payable under the policy at the same time.

Question 53:
What is the Accident Medical Expense Benefit?
Answer:
Under this Benefit, the insurance company agrees to reimburse the Insured for the actual expense of treatment by physicians, surgeons, nurses, hospital room and board charges, therapeutic charges (drugs, dressings, X-rays, laboratory fees, operating room, etc.) up to an amount not exceeding the limit specified in the policy for such expense. The maximum is a fixed amount ($500 to $10,000). The Benefit is blanket; i.e., all expenses up to the maximum are paid and the Insured is not required to be confined to a hospital to be eligible for such Benefits.

This type of coverage may be purchased under an Individual or a Group Policy. Sometimes, it is afforded by endorsement to an Accident Income Disability Policy.

This type of protection is also referred to as Blanket Accident Medical Expense Coverage.

Question 54:
Are there any other limitations?
Answer:
Yes. The expenses must be incurred because of an accidental bodily injury, and the treatment must be received within 26 weeks (52 weeks in many policies) from the date of the accident.

HEALTH POLICIES

Question 55:

Is it possible to obtain a policy which affords this type of coverage for an illness not due to an accident (Sickness Medical Expense Benefit)?

Answer:

A number of insurance companies provide a policy for the payment of medical expense on a blanket basis for illness, usually subject to a Deductible Clause and/or Coinsurance (i.e., the Insured pays a percentage of the expense, e.g., 20%, whereas the insurance company pays 80%).

Generally, an insurance company will not issue Sickness Protection except in conjunction with Accident Coverage, and the Accidental Medical Expense Benefit must be equal to (or greater than) the Sickness Medical Expense Benefit.

NOTE: Refer to Major Medical Insurance which is discussed later.

Question 56:

What other methods are used to reimburse the Insured for medical expenses under a Disability Income Policy (Medical Expense Coverage)?

Answer:

There are three other methods:

a. *Increased Income Benefit:* The Income Benefit is increased by 50% (or 100%) if the Insured is confined to a hospital. Usually, the maximum period for this increased Benefit is 52 weeks. Generally, this method is used for policies insuring only against accidents and which do not cover the Insured's family.

b. *Monthly or Weekly Indemnity Benefit:* Many insurance companies offer Medical Expense Coverage as a Monthly or Weekly Benefit (e.g., $200, $400, or $1,000 per month or $50, $100, or $200 per week). If the Insured is confined to a hospital, this Benefit is paid subject to a specified number of months or weeks. It is not related to the hospital charges actually incurred or to any other coverage which the Insured may have.

NOTE: Generally, additional indemnity (on a per diem basis) for hospital confinement (accident and/or sickness) is limited to a specific period of time, e.g., 26 weeks, 52 weeks, etc. Many policies also include such Benefits for dependents. Some insurance companies offer this coverage as an endorsement. If the policy is Noncancellable and Guaranteed Renewable, all preselected optional Benefits also become Noncancellable and Guaranteed Renewable.

The Monthly or Weekly Indemnity Benefit is designed to supplement other coverages or provide funds for frequently incurred nonmedical expenses (e.g., baby-sitters, housekeeper, etc.). Coverage is available on an Individual or a Family basis.

c. *Hospitalization Insurance Benefit:* This is the most common method of affording medical coverage. Generally, the policies are written to

HEALTH POLICIES

afford coverage for sicknesses as well as accidents for the Insured and his family. The Benefits are divided into two categories, i.e., Hospital Room and Board Charges, and Other Hospital Charges (sometimes called Extra Hospital Expenses Benefit, Therapeutic Hospital Expenses Benefit, or Miscellaneous Hospital Expenses Benefit).

1. Hospital Room and Board Charges Benefit: Coverage is afforded for a specified sum (e.g., $20, $50, $100, or $150 per day) for the payment of the hospital charges for room and board. The policy specifies the duration of the Benefit, generally 31 to 365 days. The Insured is reimbursed for the actual charges made by the hospital not to exceed the Specified Room and Board Benefit. If the Benefit were $100 per day and the hospital charges were $90 per day, the insurance company would pay $90 per day. The amount of the Benefit selected should not be less than an amount equal to the normal semiprivate room charges in the area.

2. Other Hospital Charges Benefit: Most Hospitalization Policies afford coverage for the cost of services and supplies used by a patient (e.g., X-ray equipment, laboratory tests, use of operating rooms, drugs, and dressings) provided that the Insured is a bedpatient in the hospital. If the Insured is treated in the outpatient section, the policy pays for these services if the treatment is necessitated by an accident and the treatment is considered first aid. Generally, Sickness Coverage is not afforded on an outpatient basis.

The Benefit may be *blanket,* i.e., an amount specified in the policy payable for all of the hospital charges. This amount is expressed in one of two ways, i.e., a specified dollar amount, e.g., $100, $200, etc., up to $2,000 or a sum equal to 5 times, 10 times, or 20 times the Room and Board Benefit. Thus, if the Room and Board Benefit is $50 per day and the policy specifies that payments will be made on the basis of 20 times the cost of Room and Board, the maximum Other Hospital Charges allowance would be $1,000.

The Benefit may be *allocated,* i.e., the policy may specify the amount of money that will be paid for each of the services, e.g., use of operating room — $40, X-rays — $10 each, etc.

Many policies cover the cost of a local ambulance not exceeding a specified amount (e.g., $25).

Some policies afford protection for the payment of the administration of an anesthetic administered by a private physician.

Most policies afford coverage for the transfusion of blood or plasma under the Other Hospital Charges Benefit. Some insurance companies afford coverage for the payment of blood as well; however, many policies do not cover services or supplies that may be donated or obtained free by the Insured (e.g., blood).

Some insurance companies afford protection for Service Benefits instead of Indemnity Benefits, e.g., semiprivate accommodations for

HEALTH POLICIES

31 days regardless of the charge. Under such policies, the other hospital charges are usually paid in full for this period.

Some policies afford coverage on a Coinsurance Basis. The insurance company pays 75% (or 80%) of the expenses subject to a maximum of $1,000, $1,500, or $2,000. The Insured pays the remaining expenses (25% or 20%).

In some policies, the first $200 or $300 of expenses are covered in full with the Coinsurance (Insured Percentage) applicable only to the balance subject to a maximum reimbursement of $1,500, $2,000, or $2,500.

Question 57:
What is the purpose of the Coinsurance Provision?

Answer:
According to the Coinsurance Provision used in Health Insurance Policies, the Insured is required to share the loss regardless of the amount of coverage and the amount of expenses incurred. The purpose of this provision is to eliminate the use of unnecessary medical services by the Insured, thereby reducing the cost of the insurance. Usually, the Coinsurance percentages are 75%-25% or 80%-20%, the insurance company paying the higher amount in each case.

Question 58:
Is Medical Expense Coverage limited to Accident Benefits?

Answer:
The first two methods of providing Medical Expense Coverage, namely, all expenses up to a certain amount (Accident Medical Expense Benefit), and the Increased Income Benefit are limited to accident claims. The Weekly Indemnity Benefit and the Hospitalization Insurance Benefit may be limited to just sickness cases or just accident cases, or may include both types of disabilities.

Question 59:
Is coverage afforded for the use of the services available in a Convalescent (Nursing) Home?

Answer:
An ever-increasing number of insurance companies are affording coverage for care in a Convalescent Home. Generally, the Benefits for Convalescent Home Care are more limited than for the services that are rendered in a regular hospital.

A Convalescent Home is defined as an institution whose purpose is curative rather than custodial and which provides the following services: registered nursing care, a physician on the staff who is available on a 24-hour basis, facilities for a specified number of patients (usually more than four). Furthermore, it must be licensed by the appropriate authority.

HEALTH POLICIES

Question 60:
What provision is made for the payment of surgeons' and doctors' bills?

Answer:
If the Income Benefit is increased because of hospital confinement or if the Hospital Room and Board Charges Benefit is provided, the policy may contain a Surgical Schedule and a Physicians' Expense Benefit. Usually, surgical allowances are itemized on a Surgical Schedule and are attached to a Hospitalization Policy as an endorsement (Rider). In lieu of Surgical Benefits, medical payments may be paid on a per call or per day basis. Some insurance companies afford coverage for both surgical and medical expenses which were incurred at the same time and which are due to the same disability.

Question 61:
What is a Surgical Schedule?

Answer:
A Surgical Schedule is a list appearing in the policy which indicates the amounts payable for those surgical operations which are performed most frequently. Obviously, it is not feasible to mention every possible surgical operation in the Surgical Schedule. Generally, the policy states that the payment for an operation which is not listed will be made on a basis consistent with the Surgical Schedule for comparable operations (based on the judgment of the insurance company). The amount allowed depends on the nature of the operation. Naturally, more money is paid for major operations than for minor operations. For example, the policy may contain Maximum Benefits of $200, $250, $300, or ... $3,000. The operation may take place in the doctor's office, at home, or in a hospital.

NOTE 1: Under Group Health Insurance Policies, many insurance companies are no longer relying on a Surgical Schedule, instead they pay reasonable and customary surgical charges.

NOTE 2: Surgical Schedules specifying high Benefits (generally found in Major Medical Policies) are also restricted by the "regular and customary charges" in the locality where rendered.

Question 62:
What is the Physicians' Expense Benefit?

Answer:
Some policies afford coverage for the payment of physicians' expenses. The most common method is to allow $3, $4, or ... $10 per day for each day the Insured is confined to a hospital in nonsurgical cases. If the Insured were in the hospital for 10 days and the daily allowance were $5, he would receive $50 for the payment of his physician's bill. This is called In-Hospital Medical Expense Benefit.

Many Comprehensive Plans afford coverage for visits made to a doctor's office or for a doctor's visits to the patient's home; and for other medical expenses such as prescriptions and surgical appliances. If cov-

HEALTH POLICIES

erage is afforded, generally, the cost of the first two or three visits is not covered, or the patient must be disabled (unable to work) for three or four days before he becomes eligible to collect for this Benefit.

Question 63:
If the Insured has two doctors (e.g., a surgeon and a family physician) may he collect under the Surgical Schedule and the Physicians' Expense Benefit for the bills received from both doctors?

Answer:
Most insurance companies pay the Surgical Benefit but not the Physicians' Expense Benefit unless the treatment received from each of the doctors is for a different condition. However, some insurance companies pay a surgeon in accordance with the Surgical Schedule of Benefits and a physician (other than the surgeon or his assistant) in accordance with the Physicians' Expense Benefit Insuring Clause for treatment received prior to the surgery even if the treatment rendered was for the same or a related cause.

Question 64:
Is coverage afforded for the services of registered private nurses?

Answer:
Some policies afford coverage for nursing care. These policies establish the dollar allowance on either a daily or per shift basis for a maximum number of days or a maximum dollar allowance. The Benefit is not always limited to hospital confined cases, but is payable for visiting nurse expense as well. The duties of the nurse must be limited to the care of the patient (no general housekeeping duties). The Benefit is not payable if the nurse(s) is a member of the Insured's family or normally resides at the home of the Insured.

NOTE: Generally, practical nurses are not covered; however, some policies afford coverage for practical nurses at 50% of the allowance for a registered nurse. Some insurance companies (by administrative practice) allow full Benefits for licensed practical nurses if graduate registered nurses are not available.

Question 65:
With respect to Medical Care Coverage, is an Insured limited to a certain number of Benefit Days each year or each policy period?

Answer:
No. Most policies afford coverage on a per claim basis, and not on an annual or policy period basis. For example, if a policy provides payment for 90 days of hospitalization, the insurance company might pay for 180 days if the Insured were hospitalized twice during the year for different reasons.

Question 66:
What is considered as a continuing disability?

HEALTH POLICIES

Answer:

If an Insured had not recovered completely from an illness and was receiving treatment therefor, it would be considered as a continuing disability and would be treated as one claim even if two (or more) hospital confinements were involved.

Usually, policies specify that two confinements are considered as one confinement unless the reasons for the confinements are completely unrelated or are separated by a specified period (e.g., 30, 60, or 90 days).

If a person suffering from an illness develops another illness (not similar to the first) because of his "run-down" physical condition, some insurance companies may consider both confinements as one illness if the period of time elapsed between one illness and the other is less than that stipulated in the policy.

Question 67:
Is coverage afforded for maternity cases?

Answer:

Most Family Hospitalization Policies cover maternity claims. Because this coverage is generally bought by people in the child-bearing years and since during those periods the birth rate is high, the Benefit is limited. Usually, the Hospital Expenses are covered up to 10 times the daily Room and Board Benefit. The Insured would receive $200 if the daily Room and Board Benefit were $20. This item ($200) would be paid if the hospital charges were equal to (or greater than) this amount regardless of the length of time the patient was in the hospital.

Usually, the Surgical Schedule contains a specified sum which is allowed for obstetrical expenses in addition to the Hospital Expense Benefit.

If the Insured has a miscarriage or if a birth involves surgery, e.g., Caesarean section or ectopic pregnancy, some insurance companies pay for the cost of the regular Room and Board and Extra Hospital Expense or pay a higher obstetrical Benefit.

Generally, a policy issued to cover a single individual does not cover a maternity claim, although some insurance companies provide such coverage for a married woman under a policy issued to her, for an additional charge. (Note: Some policies cover maternity claims and abortions for unmarried women.)

Question 68:
Is protection afforded for dental care?

Answer:

Normal dental care (examinations, X-rays, fillings, cleanings, extractions, etc.) is not covered under a Health Policy.

If an extraction requires surgery and confinement in a hospital, many policies provide regular Hospitalization Benefits.

HEALTH POLICIES

NOTE: Many insurance companies now afford coverage for oral surgery whether or not performed in a hospital.

The Accident Medical Expense Benefit is payable only if an accident results in injury to sound natural teeth.

A number of privately sponsored prepaid Dental Care Programs are available. Protection is afforded mainly under group practice and clinic type plans.

Dental Service Insurance Companies and Health Service Organizations are operating in this field. Numerous insurance companies afford dental insurance under Group Programs and some have developed programs which are offered on an Individual or Family basis.

Currently, Group Plans cover procedures such as oral examinations, dental X-rays, routine cleanings, fillings, extractions, oral surgery, anesthesia, treatment of peridontal diseases, root canal therapy, and orthodontics. Some plans are comprehensive and cover all or most of the cost of such treatments, while others are limited to basic dental services.

Question 69:
What is the Double Indemnity Provision, and how is it applied to Accident Coverage?
Answer:
All the Benefits except Medical Expense are doubled, namely, the Death, Dismemberment and Loss of Sight, Total and Partial Disability Benefits, and Elective Indemnities. This is done if the Insured sustains bodily injury under any of the following circumstances:

a. While a passenger in or on a public conveyance provided by a common carrier for passenger service (including the platform, steps, or running board of such conveyance). The Double Indemnity Clause does not apply to aircraft accidents.

b. If the Insured is injured by the collapse of the outer wall of a building or the burning of a building provided that the Insured is therein at the time of the collapse or at the inception of the fire.

c. By explosion of a steam boiler.

d. By hurricane or tornado.

e. By a stroke of lightning.

f. While a passenger in a passenger (not freight) elevator (excluding passenger elevators in mines).

Question 70:
What are the common exclusions or limitations applicable to Accident Coverage?
Answer:
The most common exclusions are as follows:

a. Suicide or attempted suicide while sane or insane.

b. Hernia of any type.

HEALTH POLICIES

NOTE: For many years a hernia has been considered a congenital weakness. In the past, Workers' Compensation Boards refused to honor claims for hernia operations and related unemployment. However, today almost all States recognize it as a compensable claim. In addition, most States require that if an employee is injured on the job, he must file with the Workers' Compensation Carrier and not with Hospitalization and Major Medical Carriers, in order to protect his rights relating to an "on the job" accident. He is required to clearly establish the precise circumstances under which the hernia was caused.

c. Any loss caused by or contributed to by disease or medical treatment therefor, except a bacterial infection which occurred through an accidental cut or wound.

NOTE 1: If a policy affords coverage for both accident and sickness, claims excluded under paragraphs "b" and "c" would be paid under the Sickness Insuring Agreement.

NOTE 2: Some Noncancellable and Guaranteed Renewable Policies do not contain exclusion "a".

d. War or any act of war.

e. While the Insured is in any armed forces (land, sea, or air) of any country at war. In such event, the Unearned Premiums are refunded on a Pro Rata Basis.

NOTE 1: Some Noncancellable and Guaranteed Renewable Disability Income Policies afford coverage while the Insured is serving in the armed forces except for "disability resulting from war or an act of war, declared or undeclared" or disability incurred while engaging in military aviation.

NOTE 2: Some insurance companies, which do not afford this coverage, refund the Premiums based upon the period of time that the Insured was in the service.

f. Aircraft accidents, except as a fare-paying passenger on a Scheduled Air Line.

NOTE: The wording of this exclusion is not the same in the policies of all insurance companies. Generally, insurance companies limit the coverage to Scheduled Flights. However, some extend coverage to any aircraft provided that the Insured is not operating or learning to operate the aircraft at the time of the accident.

Question 71:
Are there any other exclusions in an Accident Policy?
Answer:
These are the principal exclusions (with variations) found in most of the "Broad Form" Accident Policies.

NOTE: The "Limited Form" of Accident Policy (which will be discussed later) restricts the coverage to specific accidents, e.g., automobile, aircraft, etc.

HEALTH POLICIES

Question 72:
What are some of the exclusions and limitations applicable to Sickness Coverage?

Answer:
The most common exclusions and limitations are:

a. Pre-existing conditions, i.e., diseases or illnesses which were contracted before the policy went into effect (subject to the Incontestable Clause).

b. Disease contracted while in the armed forces of any country at war. A proportionate amount of the Unearned Premium is refunded on a Pro Rata Basis.

NOTE: Refer to the Note modifying paragraph "e" in Question 70.

c. Accidental bodily injuries.

d. Pregnancy, childbirth, or miscarriage.

NOTE: This exclusion does not appear in a Family Hospital Policy providing Maternity Benefits.

e. Diseases of the female reproductive organs.

NOTE: Most insurance companies no longer use exclusion "e". It is found chiefly in policies which have been in force for some years.

f. Many insurance companies exclude sickness or disease contracted or sustained outside of the United States, Canada, or Mexico.

NOTE: Most insurance companies which use this exclusion will issue a temporary Travel Endorsement if the request is made in writing prior to taking a trip. Most Noncancellable Health Policies do not contain any travel restrictions (or the travel limitations are not extensive).

g. Many insurance companies exclude the cost of treatment covered under a Workers' Compensation or Occupational Disease Law, and treatment or service received in any Veterans' Administration or other Governmental hospital. This exclusion applies to Hospitalization and Medical Expense Coverage. However, most Individual Policies affording Income Benefits and some of those providing coverage for hospital, surgical, and medical expenses, pay such Benefits in addition to any of the aforementioned Benefits a worker may be entitled to receive.

Question 73:
Are these sickness exclusions uniform with all insurance companies?

Answer:
No. However, they are representative of sickness exclusions found in most policies.

MISCELLANEOUS PROVISIONS

Question 1:
What are the Miscellaneous Provisions?

Answer:
Most policies contain a section in which the following clauses appear: Waiver of Premium, Assignment, Recurrent Disability, Reduction of Benefits, Mutual Policy Conditions, and, in some Hospital-Surgical Policies, a Definition of Dependents and Nonduplication Provisions.

Question 2:
What is a Waiver of Premium Provision?

Answer:
A Waiver of Premium Provision relieves the Insured of the obligation of paying Premiums if he has been Totally Disabled for a period of at least three months (six months in many policies) prior to the date the Premium becomes due and while the Insured remains continuously Totally Disabled.

Under a Disability Income Policy, some insurance companies waive Premiums only during the Benefit Period; whereas, others continue to waive Premiums as long as the Insured is disabled (even if such period extends beyond the Benefit Period).

NOTE: Most Noncancellable and Guaranteed Renewable Disability Policies contain a 90-day Waiver of Premium Clause. According to the Refund and Retroactive Provision of some policies, if a disability lasts for 90 days during which a Premium became due, the payment of such Premium is waived. Any Premium which has been paid during that period will be refunded. Some insurance companies refund the Premium in full; whereas, others refund it on a Pro Rata Basis. If the Insured should return to work during such period, some insurance companies require him to pay a Pro Rata Premium until the next regular Premium payment is due. Others, continue the Waiver of Premium in effect until the next Premium due date.

Question 3:
Is the Waiver of Premium Provision found in all policies?

Answer:
No. However, this provision appears in many policies.

Question 4:
What is an assignment?

Answer:
Legally, the insurance company must pay the Benefits to the Named Insured, his Beneficiary, or his estate. To enable the insurance company to pay the Benefits to the hospital and/or physician (on behalf of the Insured) an assignment must be made. The assignment enables the insurance company (under certain conditions) to pay the Benefits of the policy to a third party.

MISCELLANEOUS PROVISIONS

Question 5:

What must an Insured do to have an assignment accepted by the insurance company?

Answer:

The insurance company usually requires the Insured to make the assignment in writing and file it with the insurance company prior to the payment of any Benefit. The insurance company does not assume any responsibility for the validity of the assignment. In most cases, this assignment is made on the claim form at the time a claim is submitted.

Question 6:

Why would an Insured wish to assign his Benefits?

Answer:

In some instances (e.g., in the case of Medical Expense Policies), the Insured may be required to pay his hospital and/or doctor bills before receiving Benefit payments from the insurance company. Conceivably, this could create a hardship. Usually, the Insured requests the insurance company to pay the doctor and/or the hospital directly to avoid situations of this type.

An assignment of Benefits is not required by Blue Cross and Blue Shield Insureds. It is automatic. Blue Cross and Blue Shield have contracts with hospitals and doctors and all their Insureds are bound by those contracts (i.e., prepaid hospitalization, medical, and surgical plans). All private insurance companies have contracts with their Insureds and must pay them directly unless the Insured has assigned the Benefits to a hospital or a doctor.

NOTE: To facilitate the handling of claims and reduce paper work, the Health Insurance Council recommends the use of the National Information Card Plan (N.I.C.P.). Wallet size cards which are issued to Insureds contain the insurance company's name, address, phone number, and the policyholder's name and policy number. The information on this card should be made available to the hospital upon admission. Any additional information the hospital requires may be obtained by communicating with the insurance company. Under this plan, if the Insured prefers to assign his Benefits directly to the hospital, he must complete an authorization form.

Question 7:

May an Insured assign his Income Benefits?

Answer:

Yes. For example, an Insured might want to assign his Income Benefits to his employer because he is receiving his full wages from his employer while he is disabled (e.g., he has employer sponsored coverage).

Question 8:

Must the Insured assign his Benefits to his employer if he receives his salary?

MISCELLANEOUS PROVISIONS

Answer:

No. He may collect both his salary from his employer and income payments under his Health Policy.

Question 9:
Do Health Policies have a Subrogation Clause?

Answer:

No. Under most Individual Policies (Health and Disability Income), an Insured is entitled to receive the full Benefits in addition to Workers' Compensation or Non-Occupational Disability Benefits, or any other recovery as a result of injuries occasioned by the negligence of another party (either from such party or his insurance carrier).

NOTE: Some insurance companies exclude (under a Health Policy) the payment of Medical Expense Benefits which are payable under Workers' Compensation Laws. However, they often augment compensable claims if a claimant incurs medical expenses in excess of the amount collected under a Workers' Compensation Policy.

Question 10:
What is a Mutual Policy Conditions Clause?

Answer:

It is a provision which states that the policy is nonassessable. The Insured may share in the profits of the insurance company in the form of Dividends, but he will not be taxed for any excess losses or expenses the insurance company may sustain.

Question 11:
What is the Recurrent Disability Clause?

Answer:

This is a clause (used chiefly in Noncancellable and Guaranteed Renewable Polices) which states that if the Insured suffers a recurrence of Total Disability from the same or a related cause, the second period of disability is considered a continuation of the first unless the Insured has returned to work for a specified period (e.g., six months).

According to the policies of some insurance companies, the phrase "return to work" means return to the Insured's original occupation; whereas, other policies specify return to any gainful occupation for which the Insured is suited by education, training, experience, and prior economic status.

Question 12:
What is the Reduction of Benefits Clause?

Answer:

Some insurance companies reduce the Benefits by 10% per year starting with age 60, whereas others reduce them by 50% at age 65.

MISCELLANEOUS PROVISIONS

Some insurance companies terminate the policy at age 65, whereas others permit it to continue in force to supplement Medicare. Sometimes the Premium is reduced on these policies.

Question 13:
Why is the Reduction of Benefits Clause used?

Answer:
As the Insured becomes older, the frequency and severity of illnesses and injuries increase. The insurance company must either raise the rates or reduce the Benefits, unless the policy was issued on a Level Premium Basis under which the expected increase in claims was anticipated.

Generally, this provision is used in Noncancellable and Guaranteed Renewable Policies since the coverage may not be terminated by the insurance company.

Question 14:
What is the Definition of Dependents Clause?

Answer:
This clause describes who will be considered as dependents of the Insured.

Question 15:
Who are considered dependents?

Answer:
Dependents include the spouse (unless legally separated), and unmarried children under 19 years of age. (Some insurance companies include unmarried children to age 23 if they are full-time students.) The term "children" includes natural, adopted, and foster children provided that they are dependent upon the Insured for support and maintenance.

Question 16:
What is meant by "foster children"?

Answer:
Usually, the term "foster children" means any children residing in the household of the Insured, who are being reared by the Insured and who are dependent on the Insured for support and maintenance. For all intents and purposes, the Insured is considered as the children's parent even though no actual legal status (adoption) has been given to the relationship. For example, after the death of a child's parents an aunt may raise the child as her own.

Question 17:
Do all insurance companies cover foster children?

Answer:
Generally, insurance companies afford coverage for foster children. However, a few limit coverage to natural children, stepchildren, and legally adopted children.

MISCELLANEOUS PROVISIONS

Question 18:
Are any policies written to cover children over age 19?
Answer:

Yes. Many insurance companies provide coverage for unmarried children who are full-time students at accredited schools up to the age of 21, 23, or 25. This is particularly true with regard to Major Medical Policies.

NOTE: In many States the Insurance Law requires that unmarried children who are incapable of self-sustaining employment due to mental retardation or a physical handicap must be continued as dependents under Family Coverage regardless of their age.

Question 19:
Are newborn infants covered?
Answer:

Newborn infants are covered in one of three ways:

a. From birth for all expenses including nursery expenses.

b. From birth, excluding normal nursery expenses.

c. From 14 days of age.

Question 20:
What is the Nonduplication of Benefits Clause?
Answer:

Many insurance companies include a clause (particularly in Major Medical Policies) which reduces the Benefits payable if the Insured has another policy or policies affording similar Benefits. The purpose of this clause is to reduce the possibility of overinsurance and the possibility of an Insured profiting as a result of this overinsurance. The use of this provision makes it possible to utilize a lower Premium.

NOTE 1: Many States have enacted No-Fault Automobile Insurance Laws which afford Benefits for medical expenses and loss of income caused by motor vehicle accidents. In most of those States, the No-Fault Automobile Insurance Company is considered the primary insurer (except for certain motor vehicle accidents involving Workers' Compensation claimants).

NOTE 2: Most insurance companies utilize a Coordination of Benefits (C.O.B.) Provision to prevent the duplication of Benefits with those payable under other Group Plans if the Insured is covered by more than one Group Policy. Basically, the C.O.B. Provision provides for an apportionment of the payment of Benefits among the insurance companies involved.

Question 21:
What is overinsurance?
Answer:

Previously, an Insured was permitted and, in many cases, urged to buy more than one policy (even if the Benefits were identical) because

MISCELLANEOUS PROVISIONS

one policy (and, in some instances two policies) was not enough to cover the expenses incurred. This was particularly true in the case of Medical Expense Coverage. However, this situation has changed drastically in the past few years. Generally, a Major Medical Policy covers all expenses up to 75% or 80% of the incurred charges in excess of a Deductible Amount. If two policies are in effect, an Insured could collect $1.50 to $1.60 for every $1 of expense incurred. A Non-duplication of Benefits Provision prevents this abuse.

REQUIRED UNIFORM POLICY PROVISIONS

In June 1950, the National Association of Insurance Commissioners approved the Uniform Individual Health Policy Provisions Model Law, and recommended that all States use it to replace the old Standard Provisions Law.

All Health Policies must contain 12 Uniform Provisions which, in essence, cover the same ground as the previous 15 Standard Provisions; i.e., rights and duties of the policyholder and the insurance company, claim procedure, and other conditions of the policy. As in the case of the Optional Provisions under the Standard Provisions Law, there are 11 Optional Provisions under the Uniform Policy Provisions Law which cover the same material. The language of the provisions must be substantially as it appears in the Law. The following questions pertain to such Uniform Policy Provisions:

Question 1:
What must the policy contain, and how may it be changed?

Answer:
According to the Entire Contract; Changes Provision (Provision 1), the policy must contain the entire contract including endorsements and a copy of the application. A change is not valid until approved by an executive officer of the insurance company, and an appropriate endorsement is attached to the policy.

Question 2:
Is there a time limit for denying liability?

Answer:
Yes. According to the Time Limit on Certain Defenses Provision (Provision 2), the policy must be incontestable after two years have elapsed from the date the policy was issued, except with respect to fraudulent misstatements in the application. (In some States it is three years.) After the policy becomes incontestable a claim may not be denied on the basis that a disease or physical condition had existed prior to the inception of the policy.

NOTE: In Noncancellable and Guaranteed Renewable Policies, some insurance companies omit the reference to fraudulent misstatements so that the policy becomes fully incontestable (usually, after 2 years, sometimes, after 3 years), i.e., with respect to any statement made by the Insured in the application.

Question 3:
Is there a Grace Period applicable to the payment of the Premium?

Answer:
A Grace Period is the period of time following the date upon which a Premium was due during which coverage is continued. According to the Grace Period Provision (Provision 3), policies must have the following Grace Periods: a Weekly Premium Policy, 7 days; a Monthly Premium Policy, 10 days; and 31 days for all others.

REQUIRED UNIFORM POLICY PROVISIONS

NOTE: A policy in which the insurance company reserves the right to refuse any renewal must state that the insurance company will give the Insured 30 days' notice of its intention not to renew.

Question 4:
Under which circumstances may a policy be reinstated?
Answer:
According to the Reinstatement Provision (Provision 4), if the insurance company does not require a reinstatement application when a policy has lapsed, the policy is reinstated upon the acceptance of the Premium by the insurance company or its authorized agent. If a reinstatement application is required, the policy is reinstated automatically as of the date the reinstatement application is approved, or if action is not taken by the insurance company within 45 days following the date of a Conditional Receipt, the policy is reinstated automatically at the conclusion of such period.

A Premium may not be applied to any period more than 60 days prior to the date of reinstatement.

Coverage for accidents becomes effective immediately upon reinstatement.

Coverage for sicknesses does not become effective until the conclusion of a 10-day Probationary Period.

Question 5:
How soon must a Notice of Claim be given?
Answer:
According to the Notice of Claim Provision (Provision 5), a written Notice of Claim must be given to the insurance company within 20 days after the occurrence or commencement of a loss, or as soon thereafter as is reasonably possible.

If a policy provides Loss of Time Benefits which are payable for at least two years, the insurance company has the right to require that a Notice of Claim be completed by the claimant every six months.

Question 6:
Is the insurance company required to supply Claim Forms?
Answer:
Yes. According to the Claim Forms Provision (Provision 6), the insurance company must furnish a Claim Form for filing a Proof of Loss upon receipt of a Notice of Claim. If the insurance company fails to furnish such forms within a 15-day period, the claimant may write a letter giving the details of the occurrence, character, and extent of the loss for which a claim is made. This will fulfill the requirements of the policy.

Most insurance companies furnish Claim Forms promptly. If the insurance company's form is used it is more likely that all of the desired pertinent information will be obtained thus enabling it to evaluate the claim more quickly and intelligently.

REQUIRED UNIFORM POLICY PROVISIONS

Question 7:
How soon must the claimant file a Proof of Loss?

Answer:
The Proof of Loss Provision (Provision 7) states that the claimant must furnish the insurance company with a written Proof of Loss at its office within 90 days after the termination of any period for which the insurance company is liable for periodic payments, or in the case of a specified loss, within 90 days after the date of the loss. Failure to give such notice does not invalidate a claim if it can be shown that it was not reasonably possible to give such notice within the required period, provided that notice is given not later than one year from the date a Proof of Loss was required. Legal incapacity is excepted.

Question 8:
When are Benefits payable?

Answer:
The Time of Payment of Claims Provision (Provision 8) specifies that Benefit payments, other than periodic payments, are paid upon receipt of an acceptable written Proof of Loss. Periodic Indemnity Benefits are payable at least monthly. The balance remaining unpaid at the termination of a claim is payable upon receipt of an acceptable written Proof of Loss.

Question 9:
To whom are Benefits paid?

Answer:
According to the Payment of Claims Provision (Provision 9), indemnities for loss of life are paid to the Designated Beneficiary. If a Beneficiary is not designated, or if the Beneficiary is deceased, payment is made to the estate of the Insured.

Any other accrued indemnities unpaid at the time of the Insured's death will be paid either to the Beneficiary or to the estate, at the option of the insurance company.

If the Insured is living, all indemnities (unless assigned by the Insured) are payable to the Insured.

NOTE 1: The policies of some insurance companies provide that if the Insured or the Beneficiary is a minor, or legally incompetent, or if a Beneficiary had not been designated, the insurance company will pay Benefits up to $1,000 to a relative of the Insured who apparently is entitled to the money. This clause is known as the Facility of Payment Clause.

NOTE 2: Many Hospitalization Policies provide for the assignment of Benefits to a hospital or a physician in payment for the treatment received.

Question 10:
Does the insurance company have the right to examine the claimant?

REQUIRED UNIFORM POLICY PROVISIONS

Answer:
The Physical Examination and Autopsy Provision (Provision 10) specifies that the insurance company has the right to examine the Insured, at its expense, as often as it may reasonably require pending the settlement of a claim, and to make an autopsy if it is not prohibited by law.

Question 11:
When may legal action be instituted?
Answer:
The Legal Actions Provision (Provision 11) specifies that an action at law, or in equity, may not be brought before 60 days have elapsed from the date a Proof of Loss was filed, and may not be brought after three years from that date.

Question 12:
May the Beneficiary be changed after the policy has been issued?
Answer:
The Change of Beneficiary Provision (Provision 12) specifies that unless the Insured designates an Irrevocable Beneficiary, the right to change the Beneficiary is reserved to the Insured. The consent of the Beneficiary is not required for the surrender or assignment of the policy, for any change in the Beneficiary, or for any other changes in the policy.

Question 13:
How may an Irrevocable Beneficiary be changed on an insurance policy?
Answer:
An Irrevocable Beneficiary may not be changed unless the Beneficiary consents in writing to the Insured's request for such change.

Question 14:
May several persons be mentioned as Beneficiaries?
Answer:
Yes. The policyholder may designate any number of persons as Beneficiaries. Furthermore, the Insured may designate one or more Primary Beneficiaries and one or more Contingent Beneficiaries.

Question 15:
What is the difference between a Primary Beneficiary and a Contingent Beneficiary?
Answer:
The Death Benefit is paid to the designated Primary Beneficiary. However, if the Primary Beneficiary dies before the Insured, the Death Benefit is paid to the designated Contingent Beneficiary.

If a Contingent Beneficiary has not been designated in the policy, the Death Benefit is paid to the estate of the Insured.

OPTIONAL UNIFORM POLICY PROVISIONS

Instead of using a particular permissible Optional Provision, an insurance company may substitute a corresponding provision of different wording (if approved by the Insurance Department) which is not less favorable in any respect to the Insured or to the Beneficiary.

Question 1:
What action does the insurance company take if the Insured changes his occupation?

Answer:
If the insurance company includes the Change of Occupation Provision (Optional Provision 1) in the policy, the insurance company has the right to prorate the Benefit if the Insured, without notifying the insurance company, has changed his occupation to one classified as more hazardous by the insurance company. However, if the Insured changes his occupation to one classified as less hazardous by the insurance company, the insurance company will reduce the Premium and return the Excess Premium collected, to the date of the change or to the anniversary date.

NOTE: The insurance company's Classification of Occupations and the Premium Rates are filed with the Insurance Department.

Question 2:
Is coverage afforded if the Insured has misstated his age?

Answer:
The Misstatement of Age Provision (Optional Provision 2) provides that if the age of the Insured has been misstated, the insurance company has the right to prorate the Benefit so that the Insured will collect only the amount that the Premium paid would have purchased at the correct age.

If the Insured's age was overstated, most insurance companies will pay the claim and refund any excess Premium.

NOTE: In actual practice, it is more likely that an age is understated; in which case, Benefits may either be reduced to those which the Premium would have purchased at the correct age, or the coverage may be denied completely if such coverage would not have been available had the correct age been disclosed at time of issue. In the latter case, the total amount of the Premiums paid would be refunded.

Question 3:
May an insurance company limit the number of policies or the amount of Benefits under two or more policies which it issues for any one Insured?

Answer:
The Other Insurance In This Insurer Provision (Optional Provision 3) provides two methods by which coverage may be limited. The first alternative authorizes the use of a provision containing a maximum

OPTIONAL UNIFORM POLICY PROVISIONS

aggregate indemnity for a particular type of coverage (voiding all excess insurance for such coverage) and requiring a refund of Premiums for such voided coverage. The other alternative is the use of a provision limiting coverage to one policy with the same insurance company. The choice may be made by the Insured (or in the event of his death, by his Beneficiary or his estate) after which the Premiums on all other policies must be refunded by the insurance company.

Question 4:
May an Insured carry duplicate coverage with other insurance companies?

Answer:
Yes. If an Insured notifies all insurance companies concerned, he may duplicate the coverage and collect under all policies. However, if he does not notify all insurance companies concerned and duplicates the coverage (under the terms of the Insurance With Other Insurers Provision, i.e., Optional Provisions 4 and 5), those insurance companies which have inserted these Optional Provisions are permitted to prorate the Benefit. Provision 4 limits the Insured to one policy for Medical Expense. Provision 5 limits the Insured to one policy for Income, and/or Accidental Death, Dismemberment, and Loss of Sight Benefits.

Question 5:
May an insurance company define what it considers duplicate coverage (i.e., Other Valid Insurance)?

Answer:
Yes. It may specify the forms of coverage it considers Other Valid Insurance under Optional Provisions 4 and 5. Without such specific stipulation, the following are not considered as duplicate insurance: Group Insurance, Automobile Medical Payments Insurance, coverage afforded by Hospital or Medical Service Organizations (i.e., Blue Cross or Blue Shield), Union Welfare Plans, Employer or Employee Benefit Organizations.

Most of the regular Health Policies being issued currently specifically exclude all or some of the above coverages. However, innumerable policies that were issued years ago (and which are still in force) do not contain such exclusions.

Question 6:
If the Benefit payable exceeds the Insured's earned income, is the Benefit reduced?

Answer:
The Relation of Earnings to Insurance Provision (Optional Provision 6), which can be used only in Guaranteed Renewable Policies and Noncancellable and Guaranteed Renewable Policies, gives the insurance company the right to reduce the Benefit on a Pro Rata Basis, and refund the Excess Premium if, at the time of disability, the Insured's Average Monthly Income or his Average Monthly Income for the two years prior

OPTIONAL UNIFORM POLICY PROVISIONS

to the disability, whichever is greater, is less than the Benefit payable. This limitation does not apply if the Benefit is $200 per month or less. Furthermore, under these circumstances a higher Benefit may not be reduced to less than $200 per month.

Question 7:
May an unpaid Premium be deducted from a claim payment?

Answer:
Yes. If the policy contains the Unpaid Premium Provision (Optional Provision 7), the insurance company is permitted to deduct from a claim payment any Premiums due and unpaid or covered by any note or written order.

Question 8:
How may a policy be cancelled?

Answer:
The Cancellation Provision (Optional Provision 8) states that a policy may be cancelled by the insurance company only within the first 90 days after the date the policy was issued, by sending (10 days prior to the effective date of the cancellation) a written Notice of Cancellation to the last known address of the Insured. The insurance company is obliged to return the Unearned Pro Rata Premium promptly.

NOTE: Usually, coverage under a Hospital-Surgical Policy terminates on the day an Insured becomes eligible for Medicare or the day he (or she) attains age 65, whichever occurs first. Generally, coverage on an Insured's dependent spouse is not terminated until the spouse is eligible for Medicare or attains age 65.

The Insured may cancel the policy at any time by notifying the insurance company of his desire to cancel and specifying the effective date of cancellation, in which case the insurance company may send a Short Rate Return Premium.

Cancellation does not prejudice any claim originating prior to the effective date of the cancellation.

Question 9:
May a provision of a policy conflict with any State statute?

Answer:
No, the Conformity With State Statutes Provision (Optional Provision 9) specifies that any provision of the policy which, on its effective date, is in conflict with the statutes of the State in which the Insured resides is amended to conform to the minimum requirements of such statutes.

Question 10:
Is coverage afforded if any injury (or illness) arises out of an illegal act of the Insured?

OPTIONAL UNIFORM POLICY PROVISIONS

Answer:

No, the Illegal Occupation Provision (Optional Provision 10) absolves the insurance company of any liability for any loss if the Insured's commission of or attempt to commit a felony was a contributing cause, or if the fact that the Insured was engaged in an illegal occupation was a contributing cause.

Question 11:

Is the insurance company liable for a loss caused by intoxicants or narcotics?

Answer:

According to the Intoxicants and Narcotics Provision (Optional Provision 11), the insurance company is not liable for any loss sustained or contracted in consequence of the Insured's being intoxicated or under the influence of any narcotic, unless administered on the advice of a physician.

OTHER REQUIREMENTS OF THE LAW

The Laws of most States also include certain other requirements which, while not policy provisions, establish ground rules to be followed by the insurance company. The following are a few of the more important provisions:

a. The entire money and other considerations must be stated in the policy.

b. The effective date and termination date must be stated in the policy.

c. The policy must be printed in type which is not smaller than ten point, without undue emphasis on any portion of the text.

NOTE: Some States require that certain policy restrictions or limitations be highlighted in larger type and/or type of a contrasting color.

d. The policy may afford coverage for only one person. However, the Insured's spouse and dependent children may be included under a Family Policy.

NOTE: The Laws of most States stipulate that a person, other than the policyholder, who is covered under a Family Policy, has the right to convert his policy if his insurance is terminated because he is no longer within the definition of the word "family", e.g., a child upon the attainment of the limiting age (e.g., 19), or a spouse upon the dissolution of a marriage.

e. Exceptions and reductions must be grouped together under a descriptive title. (Exceptions applying to one specific Benefit in the policy may be contained in that provision.)

f. False statements on the application do not invalidate the claim unless they materially affect the acceptance of the risk.

g. The policy must not contain any provisions purporting to make any portion of the charter, rules, constitution, or bylaws of the insurance company a part of the policy unless such portion is set forth in full in the policy, except a statement of rates or classification of risks or a Short Rate Table which has been filed with the Insurance Department.

h. Individual Policies must contain a stipulation regarding the maximum age limit after which the policy will not be renewed. These requirements do not apply to Single Premium Nonrenewable Accident Policies (e.g., Aviation Policies).

i. The Insured must be given ten days to examine the policy beginning with the date the policy was delivered to him. Any time during that period, he may return it to the insurance company with a request for cancellation, in which case he would be entitled to receive a full refund of the Premium he had paid.

NOTE: This requirement does not apply to Single Premium Nonrenewable Accident Policies (e.g., Aviation Policies).

j. If one-third or more of the Premium payable for a policy is allocable to Hospital, Surgical, or Medical Expense Benefits, and if a policy has been in force for two years or more, an insurance company may not

OTHER REQUIREMENTS OF THE LAW

refuse to renew a policy except for one or more of the following reasons:

1. Fraud in applying for a policy or in effecting the payment of a claim.
2. Moral hazard.
3. Overinsurance.
4. Discontinuance of a class of policies.
5. Filing a false claim.
6. Other reasons approved by the Insurance Department.

k. Notwithstanding the requirements of paragraph "j" above, an insurance company is permitted to establish an age limit, date, or period beyond which coverage will not be afforded, or the policy will not be renewed, but this restriction must appear on the first page of the policy.

l. A policy containing provisions which are in violation of the State Insurance Law will not be construed as void, but will be considered as though it conformed to the Law. Furthermore, a provision may not make the policy less favorable to the Insured than required by the Law.

m. If a policy has an age limitation which falls within the term of the policy, and for which the insurance company has accepted a Premium, the policy must remain in force until the normal expiration of the term. If the Premium is accepted by the insurance company for a period beyond the maximum age limit, the policy must remain in force for the entire period despite the age limitation.

NOTE 1: In most States, these requirements do not apply to many related coverages, e.g., Reinsurance; Blanket or Group Health Policies; Disability Benefits Law Policies; Life Insurance; Endowment or Annuity Contracts; Life Insurance Policy Endorsements which grant additional Benefits for Accidental Death, Dismemberment, or Loss of Sight, or which contain a Waiver of Premium Provision, or which afford a Special Surrender Value or Benefit in the event of Permanent or Total Disability.

NOTE 2: Usually, any ambiguities in the provisions of a policy are resolved in favor of the Insured.

UNDERWRITING

Question 1:
How does the insurance company determine who is an acceptable risk and who is not?

Answer:
The underwriter reviews the information received from several sources and decides upon the acceptability of the applicant.

Question 2:
What are the main sources of information regarding the applicant?

Answer:
The main sources are: the application, the Agent (or Broker), inspection reports, and a medical examination (or a detailed statement of health if a policy is issued without a medical examination).

Question 3:
What are Inspection Reports?

Answer:
Inspection Reports are reports about an applicant made by firms that specialize in rendering this type of service. The inspection is made by an impartial person who gathers information from the applicant's neighbors, business contacts, and in some cases, other insurance companies. The investigator checks any and all information which may have a bearing on the acceptance of the risk. One of his principal functions is to obtain as much information as possible regarding the moral background of the applicant. He tries to determine his habits, his financial position, his family background, and his reputation. These facts are as important to the underwriter as is the health or the occupation of the applicant.

Question 4:
How do the requirements of the Federal Fair Credit Reporting Act apply to insurance companies with reference to these investigations?

Answer:
The Law requires that: (a) an insurance company must inform an applicant for Health Insurance (in writing) that an investigative inspection will be conducted and that he is entitled to request additional information regarding the report; and (b) upon written request by the applicant, the insurance company must furnish information (other than medical) with respect to the nature and scope of the investigation. If coverage is denied or a higher rate is charged, the insurance company must inform the applicant that the denial or increased rate resulted from the report, in which case it must give the name of the reporting agency.

An investigative inspection or report is one involving the applicant's character, general reputation, personal characteristics, or mode of living which is obtained through interviews with neighbors, friends, associates, or others with whom the applicant is acquainted.

UNDERWRITING

Question 5:
Is the application important?

Answer:
The application is the primary source of underwriting information. The necessity of a complete, honest, and accurate application cannot be overemphasized.

Question 6:
Who completes the application?

Answer:
The applicant or the Agent (or Broker) may complete the application. Regardless of who completes it, it must be signed by the applicant. It should be written in ink. However, most insurance companies accept a typewritten application.

Question 7:
May a statement in an application be changed?

Answer:
A statement may be changed only with the consent of the applicant. The applicant may authorize the change by initialing the correction on the original application or by a letter. Sometimes, it is advisable to prepare an entirely new application containing the corrections.

Question 8:
What information does the application contain?

Answer:
The application contains a series of questions concerning the applicant: his name, address, age, height, weight, sex, occupation, earnings, beneficiary, insurance history, and medical history. This information serves as a basis for underwriting the risk.

Question 9:
Why are the answers to the questions regarding the applicant important?

Answer:
This information is used for two purposes: (a) it identifies the applicant, and (b) it serves as a valuable underwriting consideration, as explained below:

a. Age: Because of the increase in the hazard of sicknesses and accidents in the case of older persons, most insurance companies have a limit with respect to the age of the applicant.

The Premium may be a Level Premium, i.e., one which is based upon the age of the applicant when he applies for the policy; or it may be a Graduated Premium, i.e., one which increases as he grows older. Usually, this is done on the basis of 2, 5, or 10-year age groupings.

UNDERWRITING

b. Height and Weight: The hazard of sicknesses and accidents increases among people who are overweight or underweight. Extremes in either direction are undesirable.

c. Sex. The sex of the applicant is an important underwriting consideration. Usually, a woman is sick more frequently than a man; whereas, a man is more prone to become injured by an accident.

d. Occupation, Duties of Occupation, and Earnings: These factors are important underwriting considerations. A person engaged in clerical work does not have as great an accident potential as a construction worker. Furthermore, some injuries will disable a person engaged in one occupation but not one engaged in another, e.g., a broken finger will disable a dentist but not a lawyer. Therefore, an applicant is classified in accordance with his occupation and is required to pay a Premium based on that classification.

Question 10:
Why are the duties of an occupation and the earnings of the applicant important?

Answer:
The title of the occupation does not always provide a basis for classification. Because of the different duties entailed in occupations, applicants with similar titles may be classified differently. For example, an engineer may work exclusively in an office or on a construction site supervising the actual construction.

The amount of earnings is an important factor because an insurance company will not insure an individual for an amount greater than a percentage of the applicant's earned income. Usually, the Monthly Benefit under a Noncancellable and Guaranteed Renewable Disability Income Policy or a Guaranteed Renewable Disability Income Policy is restricted to 50% or 60% of the Insured's gross monthly income. However, under a cancellable type of Disability Income Policy (i.e., a Commercial Policy), the Monthly Benefit may be as high as 75% or 80% of the Insured's gross monthly income.

Furthermore, if a Monthly (or Weekly) Benefit greater than the *acceptable percentage of earned income* were available, a claimant might be tempted to malinger (i.e., to remain away from work longer than is absolutely necessary).

Question 11:
What is earned income?

Answer:
Earned income is the income the applicant receives in the form of compensation for work performed.

It does not include income from stocks, bonds, real estate, etc. It is contingent upon his ability to work.

UNDERWRITING

Question 12:
Who may be named a Beneficiary?

Answer:
The Insured may name anyone as a Beneficiary. Usually, it is one who has an insurable interest in the life of the Insured.

While insurance companies generally insist that a Beneficiary have an insurable interest in the Insured, this is not a legal requirement. The question of insurable interest arises principally when one person takes out insurance on *another* individual in which case the person who is applying for the insurance must *always* have an insurable interest in the person he is seeking to insure.

Question 13:
What is meant by an insurable interest?

Answer:
Insurable interest is a relationship between the Insured and the Beneficiary. This relationship may be one of blood, marriage, or of economic dependence, i.e., the Beneficiary would suffer an economic loss if the Insured should die.

Question 13a:
What is meant by adverse selection?

Answer:
The term adverse selection (also known as anti-selection and selection against the insurance company) is applied to the likelihood of persons who are poor risks to seek insurance. For example, a man who has been told that he has a serious illness (which may not be readily discernible to an examining physician) is generally exceptionally eager to secure Health Insurance. An impaired risk may be tempted, to a greater extent than a normal risk, to personally seek coverage and to conceal impairments which would prevent him from obtaining insurance. Because of this tendency of poor risks to attempt to obtain coverage, insurance companies are compelled to set up selection procedures so that their losses will not be excessive.

Question 14:
Why is the insurance history of the applicant important?

Answer:
The types and amounts of other Health Insurance carried is important because of the possibility of overinsurance. The applicant's over-all record with Life Insurance as well as Health Insurance is an important underwriting consideration. Acceptability to other insurance companies indicates his desirability as an applicant for this type of coverage, or for additional coverage. The applicant may have had a policy cancelled, a renewal refused, or an application for insurance declined. This would have a definite bearing on the acceptance of the risk by an underwriter. He would want to know the reasons for the actions taken by the other insurance companies.

UNDERWRITING

On the favorable side, if the applicant has a good over-all record, it definitely would influence the underwriter toward acceptance of the risk.

Question 15:
How is the health history of the applicant obtained?

Answer:
The health history is obtained by asking a series of questions dealing with the applicant's medical history; i.e., diseases, injuries, operations, etc.

The insurance company assumes that the applicant is in normal good health for his age and sex, and has a normal accident exposure for his occupation and station in life. Frequently, poor health may be the cause of a recurrence of pre-existing conditions and other complications. Furthermore, it may increase the incidence of accidents and retard recovery. If the health of an applicant is not satisfactory, he is not eligible for the same coverage as an applicant who is in good health.

NOTE: Some insurance companies include a question regarding the hobbies of the applicant. An applicant may have little or no exposure to accidents in his occupation (lawyer, banker, etc.) but he may have a high accident exposure in connection with his hobby (e.g., flying, skin diving, skiing, etc.). The type of hobby and the time devoted to it may determine the acceptance or rejection of an application for insurance, or if accepted, it may affect the rates to be applied and the coverage to be granted.

Question 16:
Is a medical examination required in all cases?

Answer:
No. If a medical examination is not required, many insurance companies use a Nonmedical Application which must be completed in addition to the regular application. The Nonmedical Application contains many questions relating to the past and present medical condition of the applicant.

Frequently, an insurance company may require further information concerning a particular condition the applicant may have noted on his application. It may be necessary to clarify or elaborate on the condition. Usually, this additional information is obtained from the applicant's physician (by mail). Sometimes, as a result of information secured from the applicant's physician, an applicant may be requested to submit to an examination by the insurance company's doctor.

An applicant may be required to submit to a physical examination by an insurance company's physician if he is applying for a Guaranteed Renewable Disability Income Policy or a Noncancellable and Guaranteed Renewable Disability Income Policy.

UNDERWRITING

Question 17:
What other information is contained in the application?

Answer:
Usually, the application contains a statement that the information given by the applicant is true and complete (to the best of his knowledge), the effective date of the policy, and the signature of the applicant. Some insurance companies include in the application a Conditional Receipt for the Premium, an authorization for a medical statement from the applicant's physician, a statement to the effect that if an investigation is made it will be conducted in accordance with the Federal Fair Credit Reporting Act, and the signature and the recommendations of the Agent (or Broker).

Question 18:
How are the recommendations of the Agent (or Broker) helpful to the underwriter?

Answer:
It is the duty of the Agent (or Broker) to make certain that the application is completed honestly and accurately. In addition, he should supply the underwriter with other valuable information. The applicant may be a friend, neighbor, or a regular client of the Agent (or Broker) for other lines of insurance. Therefore, the Agent (or Broker) may be in a position to know the moral background, business reputation, and the financial and physical condition of the applicant.

Even though the applicant is a total stranger, the Agent (or Broker) is in a position to learn many things about the applicant, from personal observation, that will be helpful to the underwriter.

Question 19:
Once all the necessary information has been obtained, what action can the underwriter take?

Answer:
The underwriter has three options: acceptance, rejection, or acceptance with limitations.

Question 20:
What is meant by acceptance with limitations?

Answer:
This may mean one of the following:
    a. Acceptance, but for a shorter duration of Benefits than requested.
    b. Acceptance with a Waiver Endorsement (Rider).
    c. Acceptance with a longer Elimination Period than requested in the application.
    d. Acceptance on a Rated (Substandard) Basis (increased Premium and/or reduced coverage).

UNDERWRITING

e. Acceptance based upon any combination of the above.

Question 21:
What is a Waiver Endorsement (Rider)?

Answer:
A Waiver Endorsement eliminates any liability on the part of the insurance company (for a specified period) for a claim based upon a disability caused by an existing physical defect.

For example, if ulcers are excluded by an endorsement, any disability or loss caused by this specific medical condition would not be covered by the policy.

Question 22:
When is a Waiver Endorsement used?

Answer:
Generally, this action is taken if the applicant is an acceptable risk but has a physical impairment (or illness) which renders him an unsound underwriting risk with respect to that condition.

Question 23:
What types of conditions require a Waiver Endorsement?

Answer:
These conditions fall into three categories:

a. Functional; e.g., a withered arm, a trick (weak) knee, etc.

b. Chronic; e.g., chronic bronchitis, digestive disorders, etc.

c. A condition from which the applicant has only recently recovered; e.g., an operation or pneumonia.

Question 24:
Does the Waiver Endorsement remain on the policy permanently?

Answer:
It may be permanent or temporary. It would be permanent if the condition were functional or chronic, and temporary if the condition were one from which the applicant has only recently recovered.

Question 25:
Is the attachment of a Waiver Endorsement an unfair practice?

Answer:
No. An insurance company should not be expected to issue insurance covering a condition, a recurrence of which is practically inevitable. The intelligent use of a Waiver Endorsement makes it possible for a person, who ordinarily would be uninsurable, to obtain coverage for innumerable other sicknesses or accidents which could disable him.

A Waiver Endorsement should be used only when the applicant com-

UNDERWRITING

pletely understands its purpose and how it operates. The Agent (or Broker) should explain carefully the reason for its use.

NOTE: According to the Laws of some States, the signature of the applicant is mandatory on a Waiver Endorsement Acceptance Form. In those States in which the signature of the applicant is not mandatory, most insurance companies require it nevertheless to clearly indicate his acceptance of its provisions.

Question 26:
What is an Elimination Period?

Answer:
An Elimination Period is the period of time between the date the disability began to the date Benefits are payable. It is also referred to as a Waiting Period. Benefits are not payable for this period. (Do not confuse this with a Probationary Period which was discussed earlier.)

Generally, protection is available on the basis of one of the following Elimination Periods: 7, 14, 30, 60, 90, 180, or 365 days.

Question 27:
How is an Elimination Period used by an underwriter?

Answer:
The underwriter may require a longer Elimination Period than requested if an applicant has a chronic condition, such as hay fever, which may disable the applicant frequently, but for short periods of time.

Question 28:
Is the Elimination Period used only as an underwriting tool?

Answer:
No. If an Elimination Period is used, the Premium is reduced. For this reason, many applicants request a long Elimination Period on both their Sickness and Accident Loss of Time Benefits. This is a very practical approach if the applicant will continue to receive his salary from his employer for a period of weeks or months while disabled. Under such circumstances, the Loss of Time Benefits should begin at approximately the time when salary payments cease.

Question 29:
What is Rated, Substandard, or Classified Coverage?

Answer:
If the risk assumed is greater than normally anticipated (e.g., an applicant may not meet the minimum standards for normal health), Rated, Substandard, or Classified Coverage is utilized by the underwriter.

NOTE: This type of policy is discussed in more detail under the heading "Classes of Policies".

CLASSES OF POLICIES

Health Insurance Policies are divided into various classes. The main distinctions are based upon the scope of coverage afforded and the type of prospects for which coverage is designed. Coverage for Accident Benefits is available under several bases. A policy which is issued to cover a doctor is different from a policy written for a student. Hospitalization Benefits for a family issued as an Indivdual Policy is different from a Group Hospitalization Policy covering all of the employees of one firm.

Question 1:
May different classes of policies have the same plan of Benefits?
Answer:
Yes. Policies in different classes may contain the same coverages; e.g., Accidental Death, Dismemberment, Income Benefits, Medical Expenses, etc.

Question 2:
What are the main classes of policies?
Answer:
The following are the most commonly accepted classifications: Commercial, Industrial, Guaranteed Renewable, Noncancellable and Guaranteed Renewable, Rated (Substandard), Over Age, Newspaper, Credit, Business Expense, Key Man, Special Risk or Limited Policies, Blanket Accident, Major Medical, Group, Small Group, Association Group, Franchise or Wholesale, and Blue Cross-Blue Shield.

Question 3:
What is a Commercial Policy?
Answer:
A Commercial Policy is issued to an individual engaged in a nonhazardous occupation. Usually, it covers both occupational and nonoccupational disabilities. The Benefits available are high and the duration of payments is long (up to lifetime). The Premiums are payable annually, semiannually, or quarterly. The insurance company retains the right to cancel or refuse to renew the coverage.

Question 4:
What is an Industrial Policy?
Answer:
An Industrial Policy is similar to a Commercial Policy, except that in the Industrial Policy, the amounts of the Benefits are lower and the duration of the Benefits are shorter. The Premiums for an Industrial Policy are payable weekly or monthly, and the coverage may be afforded on a nonoccupational basis.

Generally, an Industrial Policy is issued to a person who is engaged in a lower-paid and more hazardous occupation. The Premiums are collected at the home or at the place of employment of the policyholder. Each Industrial Sickness and Accident Agent is assigned to policyholders living in the same neighborhood ("debit").

CLASSES OF POLICIES

Frequently, insurance companies writing this type of protection issue package policies for various industrial groups, e.g., printers, machinists, etc. The only factor used in the rating of such policies is the age of the applicant, since the insurance company includes the Occupational Loadings in advance.

Question 5:

How does a Guaranteed Renewable Policy differ from a Commercial Policy?

Answer:

The Benefits payable under a Guaranteed Renewable Policy are quite similar to those found in a Commercial Policy. However, under a Guaranteed Renewable Policy, the insurance company is prohibited from cancelling the policy; and must renew it as long as the Insured continues to pay his Premium. However, the Premium is not guaranteed, and the insurance company reserves the right to increase the Premium on a class basis (but not on an individual basis).

Some policies have a Termination Clause which provides that the policy terminates when the Insured attains a specified age (e.g., 65). Many insurance companies guarantee that the policy will be renewed to age 65, but reserve the right to refuse to renew it after that age, whereas, other insurance companies guarantee that the policy will be renewed until the Insured becomes eligible for Medicare Benefits. In some Major Medical Expense Policies, the insurance company guarantees that (if the Insured should die and if dependent's coverage is afforded) the policy will be renewed for a surviving spouse until she becomes eligible for Medicare Benefits and up to a specified age for dependent children.

Furthermore, some policies contain an Aggregate Benefit Clause which limits the insurance company's liability to a specified maximum amount.

Question 6:

How does a Guaranteed Renewable Policy differ from a Noncancellable and Guaranteed Renewable Policy?

Answer:

The Guaranteed Renewable Policy and the Noncancellable and Guaranteed Renewable Policy are similar, except that in addition to guaranteeing the renewal of the policy, the Noncancellable and Guaranteed Renewable Policy also guarantees that the Premuim will not be increased.

NOTE: Many insurance companies use the abbreviated term "Noncancellable" to designate policies in which they do not have the right to refuse to renew the policy or to increase the rate.

This type of policy is used principally in connection with Disability Income Coverage.

Question 7:

Is the underwriting the same for all types of policies?

CLASSES OF POLICIES

Answer:
No. The underwriting becomes more rigid as the scope of the coverage increases. Usually, Commercial and Industrial Policies are issued without a physical examination. Many of the Guaranteed Renewable Policies are issued without a medical examination. However, some insurance companies will not issue Noncancellable and Guaranteed Renewable Policies without a physical examination.

Question 8:
What is a Rated, Substandard, or Classified Policy?

Answer:
A policy written for a person who cannot qualify for a Standard Policy because of:

a. A health impairment such as a heart condition, diabetes, cancer, and almost any other serious condition including mental illnesses.

b. Being engaged in a hazardous occupation.

c. Participation in hazardous sports.

Question 9:
How does a Rated Policy differ from a Standard Policy?

Answer:
It differs from a Standard Policy in a number of ways: the rates are higher, the Benefits may be lower, the duration of payments may be shorter.

In most insurance companies, the protection is standard for everything other than the qualified condition and usually the latter is covered after a short Elimination Period and/or for a reduced maximum period.

The Premium is increased from 20% to 200% depending upon the condition(s) involved, and in some cases, a Waiver Endorsement (Rider) is also required.

Question 10:
Is a Waiver Endorsement used in all Rated Policies?

Answer:
Generally, a Waiver Endorsement is not used.

Question 11:
Is a Rated Policy cancellable?

Answer:
The policy may be cancelled within the limits of the State Insurance Law. However, if a policy is Guaranteed Renewable or Noncancellable and Guaranteed Renewable, it cannot be cancelled except for nonpayment of Premium.

CLASSES OF POLICIES

Question 12:
Under which Federal Law is Health Insurance afforded for persons over 65 years of age?

Answer:
The Social Security Law was amended to afford Medical Care Coverage for persons 65 and over (Medicare).

NOTE: Refer to the Medicare chapter for a description of this Federal Program.

Question 13:
Is it possible to purchase Health Insurance to supplement Medicare?

Answer:
Most policies which are issued for persons over age 65 (who are covered by Medicare) afford coverage for Benefits in addition to those afforded under Medicare, such as prescribed drugs, private duty nursing, and private room accommodations.

Some insurance companies issue policies which provide indemnity payments (e.g., $100 per week) to be payable if an Insured is hospitalized. Usually, this sum is payable for a stipulated maximum period, e.g., 52 weeks. The money may be used to compensate for items not covered by Medicare, e.g., the basic Deductible; Room and Board Benefits after the 90th day; or the Insured's portion of the Coinsurance (Insured Percentage) requirements of Plan B, i.e., 20% of doctors' and surgeons' expenses while the Insured is confined in a hospital.

Question 14:
What is a Newspaper Policy?

Answer:
It is a limited Accident Insurance Policy offered by newspapers to its subscribers. The Premiums range from 10 cents to 15 cents per week for an Individual Policy to 25 to 50 cents per week for a Family Policy. The coverage may be limited to accidents that occur while traveling or include all accidents. Generally, the policy affords Accidental Death, Dismemberment, and Loss of Sight Benefits; and many policies also include an Accident Medical Expenses Benefit.

Generally, these policies are forwarded to the Insured by mail. If the policy is issued by a company whose home office is not located in the Insured's State, usually, suit can be brought against the insurance company only in its home State.

Question 15:
What is Credit Card Insurance?

Answer:
Some national credit card organizations and oil companies offer Accident Insurance for their customers. Generally, the policy contains an Accidental Death, Dismemberment, and Loss of Sight Benefit. Some also contain an Accident Medical Expenses Benefit. Usually, the coverage

CLASSES OF POLICIES

is limited to the Travel Accident Benefit. It may be extended to include the family of the Insured for lesser amounts of indemnity. The Premiums are added to the monthly statement of the credit card customer.

Question 16:
What is a Credit Policy?
Answer:
A Credit Policy is issued to cover the payments of an installment loan (auto, mortgage, etc.). It affords Sickness and Accident Loss of Time Benefits. The amount of indemnity is limited to the amount of the unpaid loan installments. It may be written on an Individual or Group Basis. Frequently, it is arranged through the lending institution at the time the loan is granted. There is virtually no individual underwriting involved in connection with this type of coverage.

Question 17:
What is Business and Professional Overhead Expense Insurance?
Answer:
A professional man or a businessman may purchase an Income Policy to provide an income to cover his fixed overhead expenses (rent, telephone, etc.) should he become disabled. It may be purchased on a Group (Association) or Individual Basis. The indemnity payable is equal to the overhead expenses of the policyholder; or (more often) is limited to 75% of such expenses.

Question 18:
What is Key Man Insurance?
Answer:
This coverage is issued (on a Group or Individual Basis) to executives or proprietors (individuals or partners) of business firms. It may provide high indemnities (e.g., $3,000 per month) for long periods of disability (Lifetime Accident Benefit and Sickness Benefit for 5 years, 10 years, or to age 65, no confinement required). Usually, the employer pays all, or the greater part, of the Premium. Sometimes the Benefit is made payable to the employer, generally; in a case of this type, the employer continues to pay the employee his salary (in full or in part) during the disability period.

Question 19:
What is a Special Risk (or Limited Type) Policy?
Answer:
A Special Risk Policy is written to cover a specific hazard or sickness. The Benefits are limited to the specific hazard(s) covered by the policy. The following are a few examples of Special Risk Policies:

    a. Automobile Accident Policies: The coverage is limited to automobile accidents.

    b. Aviation Accident Policies: The coverage is limited to aviation accidents, which includes accidents occurring while boarding or alight-

CLASSES OF POLICIES

ing, being hit by an airplane or the propeller, exposure and/or disappearance, as well as accidents occurring while inside the plane or at the airport. The policy term may be one trip or a twelve-month period.

c. Common Carriers: The coverage is the same as the Aviation Accident Policy. However, the policy is extended to include accidents occurring on a common carrier (trains, planes, boats, buses, and taxis).

d. Sports Policies: This type of policy is written to cover the Insured while he is participating in a sport. Usually, it is written on a Group Basis covering the members of a team.

e. Snowmobile Accident Policies: These policies afford coverage for injuries sustained in connection with the use of a Snowmobile (or being struck by a Snowmobile).

f. Dread Diseases: This type of policy provides for the payment of all medical expenses incurred as a result of specified diseases subject to a stipulated maximum (e.g., $50,000).

NOTE 1: In some States (e.g., New York) the sale of Dread Disease Policies is prohibited unless basic Health Insurance Coverage is included.

NOTE 2: These are but a few of the more common types of coverage available under a Special Risk Type Policy. There are as many variations as there are hazards or illnesses.

Question 20:
What is a Blanket Accident Policy?

Answer:

A Blanket Accident Policy is a Special Risk Policy written on a Group Basis. It covers a clearly defined group of persons exposed to essentially the same hazards, such as members of a Volunteer Firemen's unit, members of an athletic team, campers at a specific summer camp, etc. Generally, such policies provide Benefits for Accidental Death, Dismemberment, and Loss of Sight, and Medical Expenses.

Question 21:
What is a Cash Value or Return of Premium Disability Income Policy?

Answer:

Under the provisions of this policy, a stipulated amount of the policy's Cash Value or a percentage of the Premiums paid is reimbursed to the Insured if the policy Benefits are not utilized (e.g., if claims do not exceed 80% of the Premiums paid by the end of a specified period of years). This coverage may also be secured by endorsement to a Disability Income Policy.

NOTE: Some States (e.g., the State of New York) have not approved the sale of this type of policy even though it appears to be rising in popularity.

CLASSES OF POLICIES

Question 22:
What is a Hospital Income Policy?

Answer:

A Hospital Income Policy (which may also be issued as an endorsement) affords Benefits on a daily basis while an Insured is hospitalized. Usually, the Benefit is a flat sum paid in lieu of any other Benefits. Frequently, this policy is offered by insurance companies which specialize in mail order insurance. However, it is also available as an endorsement to a regular Disability Income Policy.

Major Medical Insurance

Question 1:
What is Major Medical Insurance, and how does it differ from the policies previously discussed?

Answer:

Basic Hospitalization Policies are limited, and the Benefits are payable on an allocated basis; i.e., a specified sum for hospital room and board charges, surgical charges, etc.

Because of the tremendous increase in the cost of medical care, a policy free of these limitations and with higher maximum limits is necessary. Major Medical Insurance Policies (sometimes called Catastrophe Policies) fill this need. Major Medical Insurance differs from the Basic Hospital, Surgical, and Medical Programs in that generally the Benefits are not allocated, but are payable on a blanket basis. (Many Major Medical Policies pay scheduled amounts for room and board or surgery in lieu of the use of a Coinsurance Percentage. The scheduled amounts are sometimes referred to as "inside limits".)

Expenses are paid in excess of a Deductible Amount ($250, $500, $750, etc.) and equal to a percentage of the actual charges (75% or 80%) up to a specified maximum, e.g., $50,000.

Question 2:
What expenses are covered by Major Medical Policies?

Answer:

The expenses covered by Major Medical Policies are the regular and customary charges (in the locality where rendered or provided) for medical services, supplies, and treatment that are necessary and prescribed by the attending physician, including:

a. Hospital expenses for room and board and general nursing services. Some insurance companies limit the type of accommodations (semi-private) or the amount of money (e.g., $25, $50, or $100 per day).

b. Charges of physicians and surgeons. Most insurance companies require that the physician be a legally licensed physician who can prescribe drugs.

c. Charges for the services of a private registered nurse. Some insurance companies restrict this coverage to graduate nurses, others cover

CLASSES OF POLICIES

practical nurses as well. The nurse cannot be a member of the Insured's household and the services performed must be medical and not housekeeping.

Some insurance companies have a lower Maximum Benefit ($500, $1,000, $2,500) or a different Coinsurance Requirement (50%-50%) if the services are performed out of the hospital.

d. Anesthetics and fees of an anesthetist.

e. Drugs and medicines requiring a physician's written prescription and dispensed by a licensed pharmacist.

f. X-ray examinations or treatments.

g. Blood, blood plasma, and blood derivatives.

h. Laboratory examinations and tests.

i. Radiology procedures.

j. Casts, splints, surgical dressings, trusses, braces, crutches, artificial limbs, and similar orthopedic appliances.

k. Rental of hospital-type beds, wheel chairs, iron lungs, oxygen, and equipment for the administration of oxygen and other similar equipment.

l. Transportation. Most insurance companies limit the type of transportation and the distance for which they afford coverage. For example, it may be limited to local ambulance service, or to the cost of transporting the Insured by train, plane, or ambulance to a hospital capable of providing the required treatment (if such services are not available to him in a local hospital), or the coverage may be limited to a maximum amount payable (i.e., $100 to $300).

m. All other therapeutic services and supplies prescribed as necessary by a licensed physician.

NOTE: Many insurance companies extend coverage for the use of the facilities of a Convalescent Home under their Major Medical Policies. Usually, the coverage is limited to a Maximum Daily Benefit (e.g., $10 to $20 or one-half of the daily Hospital Benefit) for a specified period of time (e.g., 30 days or 90 days). Generally, the coverage is afforded if the Insured has been confined to a hospital for a period of from 5 days to 10 days prior to his admission into the Convalescent Home. In all cases, the reason for the confinement must be curative and not custodial.

Question 3:
Are these expenses paid in full by the insurance company?

Answer:
No. Usually, the policy contains a Deductible Provision and a Co-insurance (Insured Percentage) Provision.

Question 4:
What is the usual Deductible Provision?

CLASSES OF POLICIES

Answer:

The Deductible Provision varies with the type of plan. There are four basic types of plans: Flat, Integrated, Corridor, and Comprehensive.

The Deductible may apply:

a. To each cause (injury or illness).

b. To each cause during a calendar year.

c. To all causes during a calendar year.

d. To each member of the family with a Maximum Family Deductible during a calendar year.

e. To various items of expense (e.g., hospital expense, physician's expense, out-of-hospital expense, etc.).

NOTE: According to the policies of some insurance companies, if two or more persons insured under one policy are injured in the same accident, or contract the same communicable disease within 30 days, only one Deductible is applied.

Question 5:
What is a Coinsurance Provision?

Answer:

A Coinsurance (Insured Percentage) Provision requires the insurance company and the Insured to share the expense on a percentage basis. The percentages of Coinsurance vary with plans and insurance companies. The percentages used most commonly are: 75%-25%, or 80%-20%. The insurance company pays the higher percentage of the loss, and the Insured pays the lower percentage of the loss.

The main purpose of this provision is to discourage the Insured from demanding costly medical services that are not absolutely essential.

It is not unusual for a policy to include more than one Coinsurance (Insured Percentage) Provision. Many policies require the Insured to pay a greater portion of the expense for specified types of care (e.g., private nursing care or psychiatric expense if incurred out of a hospital) in order to prevent abuse of this comprehensive type of coverage.

According to the provisions of some policies, the insurance company pays the full amount of expenses incurred in excess of a specified amount ($2,000, $3,000, or $4,000); and the Coinsurance (Insured Percentage) Provision applies only to the first $2,000, $3,000, or $4,000 of expenses. There are some insurance companies that use the opposite approach (particularly under Comprehensive Policies) in applying the Coinsurance Provision, e.g., the first $1,000 of hospital expenses are paid in full, after which coverage is afforded on a Coinsurance Basis up to a stipulated maximum.

Question 6:
What is a Flat Deductible Plan?

CLASSES OF POLICIES

Answer:

A specific dollar Deductible ($300, $500, $750, or $1,000) is established. The insurance company will not pay any expense until the cost of treatment has exceeded the specified Deductible. These expenses (i.e., up to the Deductible Amount) are paid by the Insured, or he may collect in full or in part, for such portion of his expenses under his Basic Hospitalization Insurance. Medical expenses incurred for a sickness or an injury in excess of the Deductible Amount are paid by the insurance company that issued the Major Medical Insurance, usually on a Coinsurance (Insured Percentage) Basis. This is the most common type of Individual Major Medical Policy.

Question 7:
What is meant by an Integrated Plan?

Answer:

The Integrated Plan is similar to the Flat Deductible Plan with the exception that the Deductible Provision is made equal to the Benefits insured under the Basic Plan, or equal to a specified sum of money ($100 to $500), whichever is greater. The Insured must have a Basic Hospitalization Plan. The insurance company issuing the Major Medical Policy must be informed regarding the details of the Insured's Basic Hospitalization Plan. The Integrated Plan also specifies a sum of money as a Deductible Amount for those cases which are not covered by the Basic Hospitalization Program, such as out-of-hospital cases. The Deductible Amount is either the expenses paid by the Basic Plan, or the specified sum which is deducted from the payment, but not both. Usually, this type of plan is written on a Group Basis. It is very difficult to underwrite a program of this type for individuals because of the vast differences existing in their Basic Plans.

Question 8:
What is a Corridor Plan?

Answer:

The Corridor Plan is similar to the Integrated Plan except that, in addition to the Deductible Provision applicable to the Benefits insured by the Basic Plan, there is a Corridor of a specified dollar amount ($50 to $500) for which there is no insurance, and which the Insured must pay out of his own pocket.

This type of Major Medical Program pays only those expenses which exceed the Benefits paid by the Basic Plan plus the Corridor Amount. Generally, the Corridor Plan is written on a Group Basis.

Question 9:
What is a Comprehensive Plan?

Answer:

Generally, this type of plan has a small Deductible (e.g., $25 to $100). The expenses over the Deductible are paid by the insurance company or paid on a Coinsurance (Insured Percentage) Basis.

CLASSES OF POLICIES

Question 10:
Are all Comprehensive Plans identical?
Answer:
No. There are many types of programs. Descriptions of the three general types of plans follow:

a. One of the programs offered has a Deductible of $25 to $100; the balance of the medical expenses is paid on a Coinsurance (Insured Percentage) Basis (75%-25% or 80%-20%) up to the maximum.

b. Another plan also has a low Deductible ($25 to $100); the insurance company pays the next $500 (it varies from $300 to $1,000) of expenses in full. The Coinsurance (Insured Percentage) applies to any medical expenses over this amount. Some plans limit the area of full coverage (no Coinsurance) to the hospital room and board charges, or the hospital room and board charges and hospital extras (X-rays, laboratory tests, etc.).

c. A third (and latest) type combines the Basic Coverages into one package.

1. Hospital room and board charges: paid in full to $1,000 (or 80% to $1,000) subject to a dollar daily maximum (e.g., $15, $40, or $100 per day). There is no Deductible applicable to this coverage.

2. Other hospital expenses: a dollar Deductible (e.g., $25, $50, or $100) applies; the insurance company pays 80% of the remaining expenses.

3. Surgical expense: payable in accordance with a Surgical Schedule. The Maximum Benefit payable varies from $300 to $1,500. Some plans pay 80% of the expenses in excess of the scheduled allowance, others do not.

4. Medical expenses in hospital: $3 to $10 per day for doctor's visits in the hospital.

5. Other medical services and supplies (chiefly out-of-hospital expenses): subject to a dollar Deductible ($50 to $100) and payable on a Coinsurance (Insured Percentage) Basis.

Question 11:
Do these Major Medical programs have any limitations or exclusions?
Answer:
The following exclusions appear in *most* Major Medical Policies:

a. Treatment covered under Workers' Compensation or Disability Benefits Laws and treatment or service received in any Veteran's Administration or other Governmental or State Hospitals. Furthermore, many new policies exclude losses (or portions thereof) covered under the Medicare Program.

b. Charges for treatment, services, or supplies not prescribed by a legally licensed physician or practitioner of healing arts.

NOTE: Most policies require that the physician be licensed to prescribe drugs.

CLASSES OF POLICIES

c. Charges for dental care except if required as the result of an accident other than biting and chewing.

NOTE: Some policies cover extractions if hospital confinement is required.

d. Charges for eye examinations, eyeglasses, and hearing aids.

e. Charges incurred for cosmetic surgery except when necessitated by an accident or to correct congenital malformation in an infant. Generally, the plan specifies that an accident or a birth must have occurred after the effective date of the policy.

f. Charges incurred for which Benefits are payable under any other policy including Blue Cross, Blue Shield, or Group Plans.

Question 12:
Is it possible to receive Benefits under two Major Medical Policies?

Answer:
Most policies include a Nonduplication of Benefits Provision which restricts or limits the collection of a loss under each of two (or more) policies. If this provision is incorporated in both policies, the claim is settled in accordance with one of the following methods:

a. The primary insurer (the employee's carrier or the first insurance company covering the individual) pays the claim in accordance with its policy provisions. The secondary insurer (the insurance company affording dependents' coverage or the second carrier) does not pay.

b. The insurance companies prorate the Benefits according to the maximum payable under the Coinsurance (Insured Percentage) Provision.

c. Both insurance companies prorate the Benefits but do not pay in excess of 100% of the expense, in the aggregate.

d. The primary insurer pays the full Benefits based upon the terms of its policy. The secondary insurer pays the excess up to 100% of the amount of the loss.

Question 13:
Do these policies have any other limitations or exclusions?

Answer:
Many insurance companies include some of the following limitations:

a. Room and board expenses are limited to a dollar amount (e.g., $25, $50, or $100) per day or to semiprivate accommodations (sometimes semiprivate plus $3 to $5 per day).

b. A limit of $1,000, $1,500, or higher figure for surgical expenses. This may be a maximum amount or based on a Surgical Schedule.

c. Time Limit: Some policies have a Benefit Period of 1, 2, 3, 4, or 5 years. Coverage is afforded in accordance with one of the following methods:

CLASSES OF POLICIES

1. The expenses incurred within the Benefit Period are covered subject to other conditions of the policy. Benefits are not payable for expenses incurred after the Benefit Period.

2. Benefits are payable during the Benefit Period. However, a new Benefit Period may be established by satisfying a new Deductible.

d. Mental and nervous illnesses and disorders. Coverage may be restricted in a number of ways:

1. Coverage is not afforded for treatment received outside of a hospital.

2. Out-of-hospital coverage is restricted to 50% of the expenses up to a Maximum Benefit of $500 or a higher figure up to $2,500.

3. The Maximum Benefit for any mental or nervous disorder is limited to $1,000, $2,000, or $3,000 for expenses incurred in or out of the hospital.

4. Coverage is not afforded for mental or nervous disorders.

5. Out-of-hospital psychiatric care is limited to $10 per visit and 20 visits per year.

NOTE: Coverage for confinements in mental institutions is afforded if the care is curative and not custodial. In many cases, particularly with children, the reason for the confinement may be a combination of care and treatment. In these cases, the insurance company usually utilizes a formula based on what portion of the expense is incurred for treatment and what portion is incurred for custodial care and pays only that portion of the expense which is incurred for treatment.

e. Maximum Lifetime Benefit of $10,000. This limitation usually includes a Restoration of Benefits Provision which specifies that when $1,000 or $1,500 of Benefits have been paid, the Insured may restore his Maximum Benefit if he can furnish evidence of insurability satisfactory to the insurance company.

f. Accumulation Period. The Deductible must be accumulated within 90 or 180 days.

g. The Deductible is re-established if the Insured has a 3-month (or 6-month) period during which less than $50 of expenses were incurred (some policies specify any expense).

h. Private nurse expenses may be limited as follows:

1. The Coinsurance is reduced to 50%.

2. The Maximum Benefit is limited to $500 or a higher figure up to $3,000.

3. Coverage is not afforded for expenses incurred out of a hospital.

i. Pre-existing conditions are excluded. A pre-existing condition is defined as one for which the Insured is or has received treatment, or the

CLASSES OF POLICIES

condition had been diagnosed prior to the effective date of the policy. Most insurance companies limit the period for which prior treatment was rendered from 3 to 6 months.

There are several types of definitions that explain the insurance companies' obligations with respect to pre-existing conditions. Some of them are mentioned below:

1. Coverage is not afforded for any pre-existing conditions.

2. Coverage is not afforded for any pre-existing condition for which the Insured had received treatment during a specified period (e.g., 30 days, 90 days, or 180 days) prior to the effective date of the policy. However, coverage is afforded for a pre-existing condition after a specified period (e.g., 30 days, 90 days, or 180 days) has elapsed (after the effective date of the policy), provided that the Insured did not receive any treatment or medication for that condition during the specified period.

3. Pre-existing conditions are covered after a specified period (e.g., 3 months, 6 months, 12 months) even though the Insured received treatments and/or medication during the specified period.

4. Some policies afford protection in accordance with a combination of the aforementioned definitions (e.g., 2 and 3), i.e., coverage is afforded after a specified period (usually 3 months) during which the Insured did not receive any treatment, or after a longer period (usually 6 months or 12 months) if treatment was received, whichever occurs first.

j. Maternity coverage: Generally, maternity coverage under Major Medical Policies is limited to complications of pregnancy which include surgical procedures (Caesarian sections, ectopic pregnancies) but exclude normal delivery. However, Comprehensive Plans generally include a normal delivery Benefit similar to the Benefit payable under a Basic Plan.

Question 14:
What is Piggy-Back Major Medical, Excess Major Medical, and Super Major Medical Insurance?

Answer:
These are the terms used to describe the Major Medical Policies (now being offered by only a few insurance companies) which contain a very high Deductible and high Benefit limits. The purpose of the policy is to supplement other Major Medical Coverage which may be inadequate. Generally, these plans offer a $5,000 or $10,000 Deductible and have a high Maximum Benefit Limit, e.g., $100,000. Usually, Benefits are afforded on a Coinsurance Basis.

NOTE: Group and Individual Plans issued by some insurance companies contain Maximum Benefit Limits as high as $250,000 (and over) with Variable Deductibles depending upon the other basic or underlying coverages carried by the Insured.

CLASSES OF POLICIES

Group Insurance

Question 1:
What is meant by Group Insurance?

Answer:
Group Insurance is a form of insurance in which a policy is issued to cover a number of persons who have a common affiliation, such as employment or membership in an organization or association. State laws regulate the issuing of such policies, and specify the types of groups eligible, the size of the group, the persons eligible, and the number of eligible persons who must participate before a policy may be issued.

Question 2:
Which types of organizations are eligible for Group Policies?

Answer:
Any group of persons who have a common bond, such as employment or membership in an organization or association, which has been organized for some purpose other than the purchase of insurance is eligible for a Group Policy.

Question 3:
Are all the members of the Group eligible to participate in the plan?

Answer:
All persons within the classification specified in the policy are eligible. This regulation applies chiefly to employer-employee Groups. The employer may specify certain Groups as being eligible for insurance, such as only salaried employees.

Question 4:
What factors may be used by an employer to determine the classification?

Answer:
An employer may use (for classification purposes) the employees' length of employment, salary categories, position, location of employment, or duties. All persons in the classification selected by him are eligible for the insurance without discrimination.

NOTE: The Federal Law forbids discrimination because of sex. Therefore, the sex of employees may not be used as a factor in determining the classification.

Question 5:
Must all eligible employees receive the same Benefits?

Answer:
No. The Benefits may vary with the classifications.

CLASSES OF POLICIES

Question 6:
Must all eligible employees participate in the program?

Answer:
In most States, the Law requires that 100% of the eligible persons participate in the plan if it is *noncontributory;* i.e., the employer pays the entire cost. Some States exempt persons who, for religious reasons, do not wish to participate. They must waive their rights to take part in the program.

If the plan is *contributory,* i.e., the cost of the plan is shared by both the employer and the employee (or if the employee pays the entire cost) 75% of the eligible persons must participate.

NOTE: Most insurance companies require the employer to contribute to the plan.

Question 7:
Does each person participating receive his own policy?

Answer:
No. The insurance company issues one policy, called a Master Policy, to the employer and Certificates of Insurance to the protected persons (those members of the Group covered by the Master Policy).

Question 8:
How does an employee apply for insurance?

Answer:
He applies for insurance by completing an enrollment card or form.

Question 9:
Are the underwriting rules applicable to a Group Policy similar to an Individual Policy?

Answer:
No. Under a Group Policy, the insurance company must insure all eligible employees, regardless of their physical condition.

However, if the plan is a contributory one, and a newly hired employee does not elect to be covered by the Group Plan within 31 days after he becomes eligible for coverage, the insurance company has the right to require evidence of insurability from him if he applies for coverage at a later date. If an eligible person does not enroll during the 31-day period, he must prove his insurability to the insurance company by completing an application covering his health history and/or submit to a physical examination. In such case, the insurance company has the right to decline to accept him.

Question 10:
May the insurance company use a Waiver Endorsement?

CLASSES OF POLICIES

Answer:
No. The coverage may not be cancelled or restricted by a Waiver Endorsement on any individual or his dependents (if dependent coverage is afforded).

NOTE 1: The insurance company has the privilege of cancelling the Master Policy at any time, in which case there would not be any further coverage for the entire Group.

NOTE 2: Some insurance companies use Waiver Endorsements on Group Disability *Income* Policies.

Question 11:
What are the principal factors that determine the cost of the Program?

Answer:
The main factors are: the basis of the plan of Benefits (i.e., the amount and duration of Benefits) and the number of persons of each sex. The final cost of the program is determined by the losses of the Group and the expenses of the insurance company.

NOTE: If the plan is Experience Rated, the Excess Premiums (the portion above the losses and expenses) are returned to the employer as a nontaxable dividend (rebate).

The ages and wages of the members of the Group have a great bearing on the type, frequency, and duration of claims, and the charges made by hospitals and doctors.

NOTE: If a Group Plan is being rewritten by another insurance company, the Group will be required to supply the new insurance company with the Premiums and loss figures (usually for the three previous years) of the prior insurance company. If the losses are very high, the new insurance company will take this into consideration when rating the plan. In no event may the first-year rates of the new insurance company be *lower* than its Manual Rates filed with the Insurance Department.

Question 12:
What Benefits are available under a Group Policy?

Answer:
The Benefits available are virtually the same as those available under an Individual Policy, e.g., Accidental Death, Dismemberment, and Loss of Sight Benefit; Sickness and Accident Weekly Indemnity Benefit; Hospital, Surgical, and Medical Expense Benefits; and Major Medical Benefits.

Question 13:
What happens to a protected person's coverage if he leaves the Group?

Answer:
Usually, the Master (Group) Policy contains a Conversion Privi-

CLASSES OF POLICIES

lege, under which any employee or member may (without evidence of insurability) convert his coverage. Usually, he must have: (a) been insured for at least 3 months; (b) made his request within 31 days of the termination of his insurance under the Group Policy; and (c) paid at least the Quarterly Premium, applicable to the person's age, class of risk, and plan of Benefits.

Generally, the employee (or member) may select one of several plans of reimbursement. Furthermore, usually, each plan must (at the option of the employee or member) provide identical coverage for his dependents who were covered under the Group Policy, but the dependents' Benefits may not exceed Benefits for such persons under the Group Policy. The Individual Policy need not provide Maternity Benefits, and may exclude any condition excluded by the Group Policy.

Generally, a written notice of the Conversion Privilege is given to the employee (or member) within a specified number of days after the termination of the Group Coverage.

Note 1: The Conversion Privilege does not apply to Group Disability Income Coverage.

Note 2: In some States, it does not apply to Group Major Medical Coverage.

Question 14:
How large must the Group be to be eligible for a Group Policy?
Answer:
In most States, a Group Policy may be issued for two or more persons. (Note: It may be issued for one person if he is both an employer and an employee.)

Although many insurance companies issue Group Policies only to a Group of no fewer than 25, some insurance companies have programs designed for Groups of 4 to 25 or 10 to 25 persons. Even though the number of Insureds is small, it is nevertheless considered Group Insurance in that a Master Policy is issued to the employer and Certificates of Insurance are issued for the protected persons.

Question 15:
Are the underwriting rules the same as the rules for larger Groups?
Answer:
The underwriting of a small Group is not as liberal as for larger Groups, but more liberal than for Individual Policies.

Question 16:
How do the applicants of such small Groups apply for coverage?
Answer:
The applicants complete an enrollment card or form which, unlike the enrollment card of larger groups, may include a few medical ques-

CLASSES OF POLICIES

tions. If the Group, as a whole, has an adverse health history, the entire risk is rejected. Usually, if the health history is good (with only a few exceptions) the entire risk is accepted without waivers or restrictions. However, in many instances, waivers are used in connection with small Groups.

Question 17:
Can the coverage on any one individual be cancelled?
Answer:
No. The insurance company cannot cancel the coverage on any protected person or his eligible dependents as long as he remains a member of the society or is engaged by the employer. However, the coverage for the entire Group may be cancelled by the insurance company.

Question 18:
What is Association Group Insurance?
Answer:
Many insurance companies issue Health Insurance for members of a professional or trade association. While it is possible to write a Group Policy on associations of this type, it is very difficult to satisfy the participation requirements of Group Insurance (75% of the Group). The most common method of affording coverage is by the issuance of Commercial Type Policies to the participating members.

NOTE 1: Some States do not permit the issuance of Group Insurance to Professional Associations. In those States, it is necessary to insure members under Individual Franchise Policies.

NOTE 2: Association Groups are also covered under a Group Policy that was filed with the Insurance Department as an Individual Policy with modifications that apply to the Group. Under an Individual Policy, the insurance company can require a medical history with the right to make an inspection report and can reserve the right to offer or refuse the applicant coverage. Usually, unit billing (rather than group billing) is employed.

The advantage of Association Group Insurance is the low Premium and the guarantee (once in force) that it will be treated the same as a Group Program.

Question 19:
Is it true Group Insurance?
Answer:
No. A Master Policy is not issued. The participating members receive a Commercial Type Policy and not a Certificate of Insurance.

Question 20:
What are the underwriting requirements of Association Group Insurance?

CLASSES OF POLICIES

Answer:
The usual practice of insurance companies writing this type of business is to underwrite each Group based on its size and the number of members participating. On small Groups, the underwriting is rigid (i.e., the insurance company declines to issue the coverage or it uses Waiver Endorsements). However, if the Group is large and at least 50% of the members participate, the insurance company relaxes its underwriting requirements.

Applicants with conditions which would make them uninsurable or which would require a Waiver Endorsement are accepted as standard (without waivers or restrictions). Usually, this does not apply to Disability Income Policies, which may be issued with a Waiver Endorsement and/or limited amounts of coverage for certain specified individuals.

Question 21:
Is the coverage cancellable on participating members?

Answer:
No. As long as the Association Plan remains in force, the insurance company must renew the coverage on each member who maintains his membership in the association and pays his Premiums, and is engaged in the same occupation which made him eligible for membership in the association.

Question 22:
Can he convert his coverage if he leaves the Group?

Answer:
Yes. He is given the opportunity to convert to an Individual Policy.

Question 23:
Is the Premium the same as for a Group Policy?

Answer:
The Premium Rates are lower than would be applicable if the insurance were sold on an individual basis, but higher than a Group Policy.

Question 24:
Is the association expected to perform any function other than make the insurance available to its members?

Answer:
Yes. It is expected to cooperate with the insurance company in enrolling the Group, and, in some cases, to administer the plan (i.e., to bill and collect Premiums from its members and to remit them to the insurance company).

Question 25:
What is Franchise Insurance?

Answer:
This is a method of marketing Health Insurance for groups which do

CLASSES OF POLICIES

not comply with all the criteria of a Group Insurance Plan. For example, Franchise Insurance can be used in those States which prohibit the issuance of a Group Policy to members of a Professional Association. This type of contract may also be employed if: (a) the group to be covered consists of a limited number of persons, (b) the percentage of participation by the group is low, and (c) the Benefits required are more than those afforded under a conventional Group Program.

The form of policy issued is the same for the entire group, although the amounts and types of coverage may vary among the participants. Individual Policies are issued to each Insured. The group is expected to cooperate with the insurer in enrolling members and administering the plan, i.e., to bill and collect Premiums from the Insureds and remit them to the insurer. Usually, Premiums are lower (because of administrative savings) than those payable under Individual Policies but higher than under a Group Plan.

Question 26:
Why would an employer-employee group be interested in a Franchise Plan instead of a Group or a Small Group Program?
Answer:
A Franchise Plan is offered chiefly in those cases in which the requirements of Group Insurance cannot be satisfied.

Question 27:
Are these the only classes of Health Policies?
Answer:
Since it is the function of Health Policies to meet the needs of the public, it is an ever-growing and expanding form of insurance. At the present time, these are the classes of Health Policies that are available. As the need for additional forms of coverage becomes apparent, they will be developed by insurance companies.

Blue Cross and Blue Shield

Question 1:
How do the Blue Cross and Blue Shield Programs differ from plans offered by insurance companies?
Answer:
Blue Cross is a nonprofit organization which provides a prepaid service as opposed to a reimbursement type of program as written by insurance companies. Usually, the plan provides semiprivate hospital accommodations and the payment of charges made by the hospital for drugs, dressings, operating room, laboratory charges, etc. Generally, the care and treatment must be received in a hospital which is a member of the Blue Cross Association. The programs are local and vary with localities.

The Blue Shield Association is also a nonprofit organization. It provides its subscribers with a program of prepaid surgical and/or medical care. Benefits are paid in accordance with a Surgical Schedule for treat-

CLASSES OF POLICIES

ment received from a participating physician. The program may also provide for physician's expenses incurred for nonsurgical cases. Blue Shield Programs are local and vary with localities.

Insurance companies and Agents (or Brokers) do not solicit or underwrite these programs. However, Agents (and Brokers) should be familiar with the Blue Cross and Blue Shield Programs.

Question 2:
How may information be secured regarding the details of such coverage?
Answer:
The applicant must communicate with the local office of the organization.

Group Practice Plans

Question 1:
How do Prepaid Group Practice Health Plans operate?
Answer:
A few Prepaid Group Practice Plans are available. Among these are the Health Insurance Plan of Greater New York (HIP); the Kaiser Foundation Health Plans; the Community Health Association of Detroit (CHA); Group Health Association, Inc.; and the Group Health Cooperative of Puget Sound.

Generally, under these plans, prepaid preventive, diagnostic, and curative medical services are afforded through a group of medical specialists participating in the plan and working as a team(s) in a group center. The programs have been successful and are recommended as a possible solution to affording adequate universal national health care.

Question 2:
What is a Health Maintenance Organization (HMO)?
Answer:
A Health Maintenance Organization is a health care facility similar to a hospital. It is maintained by funds collected from enrollees in the organization. (Similar to prepaid group medical practice.) The emphasis of this facility is on preventive rather than curative medicine. The organization may be run by a corporation or by a group of individuals such as a group of doctors. The HMO is a relatively new concept designed to improve the delivery of health care at reasonable costs and to provide proper medical care to persons at all levels of income.

The Federal Government enacted the Health Maintenance Organization Act of 1973 to encourage the development of HMO's. This Act is under the supervision of the Secretary of Health, Education, and Welfare. In order to be considered an HMO (under this Act) it must be a legal entity which is organized and operated in a prescribed manner and which provides Basic and Supplemental Health Services to its members as required by the Act.

MEDICARE

Question 1:
What is "Medicare"?

Answer:

"Medicare" is the popular name given to the 1965 Amendments to the Social Security Act which provide a program of Health Insurance and Medical Care for the Aged. This program consists of two parts:

a. *Basic Hospital Plan (Plan A):* This Plan affords protection for hospital expenses, nursing care in a qualified posthospital skilled nursing facility, and home health services after confinement in either institution.

b. *Supplementary Medical Plan (Plan B):* Under this Plan, protection is afforded for physicians' and surgeons' fees and certain other charges which are not covered under the Basic Plan. The Supplementary Plan is available on a *voluntary* basis.

Question 2:
Who is covered by Medicare?

Answer:

Nearly everyone who attained age 65 before 1968 is eligible for hospital insurance, including people not eligible for cash Social Security Benefits. However, coverage is *not* afforded for Federal employees who are protected under the Federal Employees Health Benefits Act and persons who have been convicted of certain subversive crimes.

Individuals who have been receiving Disability Benefits (under either the Social Security Act or the Railroad Retirement Act) for at least 24 consecutive months. They are also eligible to enroll in the Supplementary Medical Plan. This provision pertains not only to disabled workers but also to disabled widows and disabled dependent widowers between the ages of 50 to 65; women age 50 (or older) who are entitled to Mother's Benefits and who for 24 months prior to the first month they would have been entitled to Medicare protection met all the requirements except for the actual filing of a disability claim; and disabled persons over 18 who receive Social Security Disability Benefits because they were disabled prior to age 22.

An individual (even though under age 65) who is Fully or Currently Insured under the Social Security Act, or a spouse or a dependent child of such individual, who requires hemodialysis treatment or a renal transplant for a chronic renal disease is deemed disabled for purposes of Medicare Coverage (Plans A and B). Eligibility begins the third month after the month in which a series of treatments for renal hemodialysis began and ends 12 months after the month in which the individual has had a kidney transplant or the dialysis treatment ends.

An individual who is age 65 and who does not meet the usual criteria for eligibility, is nevertheless eligible for Medicare Coverage if he meets both of the following requirements: (a) he is a resident of the United States; and (b) is either a United States citizen or a lawfully admitted alien (for permanent residence) who has lived in the United States for at least five continuous years.

MEDICARE

A person enrolling under these circumstances must *pay* a monthly Premium for Plan A Coverage. Furthermore, he *must* also enroll in Supplementary Plan B (and pay the *regular* prevailing Premium). If coverage under Plan B is terminated for any reason (e.g., nonpayment of Premium or withdrawal), Plan A Benefits are ended automatically. However, the termination of Plan A Coverage does not result in the automatic cancellation of Plan B Coverage.

Question 3:
When was Medicare Coverage first available?
Answer:
Medicare Coverage became effective July 1, 1966. Increases in Social Security Tax payments started January 1, 1966 for the Basic Plan. Premium payments (paid by the Insured) for the Supplementary Plan started July 1, 1966.

Question 4:
Is coverage automatic?
Answer:
All persons who were 65 years of age or older on July 1, 1966 and who were on the rolls of the Social Security or Railroad Retirement Agencies were covered automatically under the Basic Plan as of the effective date of the Plan. Those who reach age 65 after the effective date are covered on the first day of the month in which they attain age 65 if they receive Benefits under Social Security or Railroad Retirement. All other individuals including those persons who have attained age 65, but have never applied for Social Security Benefits (i.e., they may still be working) must apply for Basic Plan Coverage at a local Social Security office.

A person who is entitled to receive Benefits under the Basic Plan is enrolled automatically in the Supplementary Plan (B). If he does not want to participate in Plan B, he is given an opportunity to decline the coverage. If he declines the coverage, or subsequently withdraws from the Supplementary Plan, he may enroll (or re-enroll) during a General Enrollment Period. Coverage becomes effective July 1st of the year in which he enrolls (or re-enrolls). However, he is limited to only two re-enrollments in the Supplementary Plan.

The General Enrollment Period is conducted during the first three months of each year. If an individual did not enroll when he first became eligible, or re-enrolled after terminating his coverage, his Monthly Premium is increased by 10% for each full 12-month period in which he could have been (but was not) enrolled. In making this computation, the period to be taken into account are the months which elapsed between his eligibility date and the close of the enrollment period in which he enrolled.

All persons who are covered under Medicare receive a red, white, and blue Identification Card indicating the effective dates of their Hospital and/or Medical Insurance Coverage.

MEDICARE

Question 4a:
How may an Insured terminate his Supplementary (B) Coverage?
Answer:

An Insured may terminate his Supplementary (B) Coverage at any time by filing a Notice of Termination or by the nonpayment of a Premium. If the first alternative is chosen, termination of coverage takes effect at the close of the calendar quarter following the calendar quarter in which the Notice of Termination was filed. For example, if a notice were filed during March 1976, the termination of coverage would take effect on June 30, 1976.

Under the second alternative, coverage ends at the close of the Grace Period during which an overdue Premium could have been paid. Regulations provide for a Grace Period of up to 90 days (up to 180 days if failure to pay the Premium was due to good cause) during which an overdue Premium(s) may be paid and the coverage continued.

Question 5:
What is meant by a Benefit Period?
Answer:

A Benefit Period begins when an Insured enters a hospital and ends when he has not been an inpatient in a hospital (or a skilled nursing facility) for 60 consecutive days.

Question 6:
What Benefits are afforded under the Basic Plan?
Answer:

The following protection is afforded under the Basic Plan:

a. Hospital Coverage: Plan A contains a Deductible Provision, i.e., the Insured must pay a specified initial amount of the hospital charges for each Benefit Period up to 90 days; plus a specified amount per day from the 61st day through the 90th day. In addition to the coverage afforded for 90 days, each individual has a lifetime discretionary reserve of 60 days. This lifetime optional reserve may be utilized only after the coverage for 90 days has been exhausted. Medicare will pay all of the covered hospital expenses in excess of a stipulated sum per day during those 60 days.

The Basic Plan pays the balance for all hospital services normally furnished to inpatients (including the cost of room and board in semi-private [two to four-patient bedroom] accommodations, ordinary nursing care, and the cost of drugs and other supplies usually furnished to inpatients). Note: It does not pay for the services of physicians and surgeons, private nursing care, or for the services of hospital employed radiologists, anesthetists, pathologists, or for the first three pints of blood.

b. Post-Hospital Skilled Nursing Facility Care: Up to 100 days if the patient requires the services of an approved nursing home or a skilled nursing facility provided that the patient has been in a hospital for at least three consecutive days prior thereto and is admitted to a skilled

MEDICARE

nursing facility within 14 days of his hospital discharge (for further treatment of the condition for which he was hospitalized) or within 28 days if appropriate bed space was not available (during that 14-day period) in the geographical area in which he resides. Furthermore, the 14-day limitation is waived if an individual's condition is such that skilled nursing care would not be medically appropriate within that period and the services may be rendered at such time as it is medically appropriate to begin an active course of treatment in a skilled nursing facility. The patient pays nothing for the first 20 days. Thereafter, the patient must pay a specific daily amount and the Basic Plan pays the balance of the costs and charges for the remainder of his stay, up to 80 days.

NOTE: The exact amount that an Insured must pay toward hospital charges, and care in a skilled nursing facility has increased annually (and it is anticipated will continue to be changed frequently); therefore, the specific figures were not indicated above.

After a total of 100 days, the patient is no longer covered by the Skilled Nursing Facility Care portion of Medicare. After each Benefit Period, which may extend up to 90 days in a hospital (plus all or a part of the lifetime optional reserve of 60 days) and then possibly up to 100 days in a skilled nursing facility, payments under the Basic Plan stop until the patient has been "home" (discharged from either a hospital or a skilled nursing facility) for 60 consecutive days after which a new Benefit Period would begin. However, there is a lifetime limit of 190 days for Benefits for psychiatric hospital services.

c. Home Health Services (after discharge from a hospital or a skilled nursing facility): Up to 100 home visits per year by a nurse or technician (furnished by a home health agency during the 365 days after discharge) in accordance with a plan established and periodically reviewed by a physician. This plan must be prepared (in writing) within 14 days after the patient's discharge. There are no Deductibles, Coinsurance, or other charges for home health services under this Plan.

NOTE: The Benefits of the Basic Plan are also paid for the month of death for an eligible individual.

Question 7:
What Benefits are afforded under the Supplementary Plan?

Answer:
The Supplementary Plan pays 80% of the necessary and reasonable charges for: (a) physicians' and surgeons' services, wherever rendered (e.g., at home, or in a doctor's office, clinic, or hospital); (b) up to 100 home health visits under an approved plan each calendar year without prior hospitalization. This is in addition to the 100 visits covered under the Basic Plan. (Note: This period differs from that indicated above under Plan A.) Home health visits are subject to Coinsurance requirements.

NOTE: The Benefits are subject to a *calendar year* Deductible.

INSURANCE LAW

With few exceptions, the following explanations apply in most States. However, if your copy of the Health Insurance Primer contains a special Addendum applicable to your State, review carefully the explanations contained in the Law chapter of that Addendum and disregard the following chapter.

Question 1:
Is a violation of the Insurance Law considered a crime?

Answer:
Every violation of any provision of the Insurance Law is a misdemeanor (unless construed as a felony which is more severe). Punishment for a misdemeanor may result in a fine or imprisonment or both. This is in addition to the suspension or revocation of all insurance licenses.

A fine of up to $500 per offense (not to exceed $2,500 in the aggregate) is an example of the type of penalty which may be imposed by an Insurance Department in lieu of the suspension or revocation of licenses.

Question 2:
What is the definition of a Health Agent?

Answer:
Generally, a Health Agent is defined as any authorized or acknowledged agent of an insurance company or fraternal benefit society, and any sub-agent or other representative of such an agent, who acts as such in the solicitation of, negotiation for, or procurement or issuance of an Insurance Policy, other than as a licensed Insurance Broker. Usually, it is considered a misdemeanor for any person, firm, or corporation to act as an Agent without a license.

Generally, State laws do not apply to (a) an Agent of a fraternal benefit society, if he devotes (or intends to devote) 50% or less of his time to the solicitation and procurement of insurance policies, or (b) employees of a licensed Insurance Agent who do not solicit or accept applications or orders outside the office of the Insurance Agent, and who do not receive compensation or commission dependent upon the amount of business transacted.

Question 3:
What is the distinction between a Broker and an Agent?

Answer:
An Agent represents a particular insurance company as a licensee and is considered an Agent of the company. A Broker may place insurance with any insurance company authorized to do business in the State and in most respects is considered an agent of the Insured.

In some States, only Agents may be licensed to sell Health Insurance (not a Broker), i.e., their laws require that Health Insurance be sold only by a person who is licensed as an Agent for the insurance company

INSURANCE LAW

he represents. In many States, a person may have a Health Insurance Agent's license with one or more insurance companies and, at the same time, conduct a General Insurance business under a Broker's license.

Question 4:
May an Agent solicit for an insurance company that is not authorized to issue insurance in his State?

Answer:
A person (firm, association, or corporation) may not act as an Agent for an insurance company not licensed to do business in the State. Such solicitation could result in a monetary penalty and/or imprisonment.

Question 5:
Who may receive commissions?

Answer:
An insurance company (or person) may not pay a commission to anyone except a licensed Agent of that insurance company or to a licensed Broker. An Agent of one insurance company is prohibited from splitting his commission with the Agent of another insurance company. However, an Agent may split his commission with a licensed Agent representing the same insurance company.

A Sub-licensee acts as an Insurance Agent in accordance with a license issued to a partnership of which he is a partner, or to a corporation of which he is an officer or director. His license requirements are the same as those of an individual Agent.

Usually, a partnership or a corporation must have at least one Sub-licensee; and generally, there is no limit to the number of Sub-licenses which may be issued to a partnership or to a corporation. The only limitation that applies to such situations is that every Sub-licensee of a partnership must be a partner, and a Sub-licensee of a corporation must be either an officer or a director.

Question 6:
Why do State Insurance Departments require that Agents be licensed to sell insurance?

Answer:
The States license Agents in order to protect the public by requiring such Agents to be competent and trustworthy and to maintain professional standards of ethics prescribed by law. The right to issue a license, and to revoke or suspend a license, gives the Insurance Department adequate control over the conduct of Agents.

Question 7:
How may an applicant secure a license?

Answer:
In most States, in order to secure a license, an applicant must:

INSURANCE LAW

a. Complete an application.

b. Be certified by the insurance company he will represent.

c. Pass an examination.

d. Be at least 21 years of age at the time of the issuance of his Health Agent's license.

NOTE: The age requirement varies from State to State.

A license may be refused if the State Insurance Department believes the applicant to be incompetent or untrustworthy, or if he has failed to comply with some prerequisite.

Question 8:
How long does an Agent's license remain in effect?
Answer:
A Health Agent's license remains in effect as long as the insurance company which employs him is authorized to do business in the State unless it is: (a) surrendered for cancellation by the Agent, (b) suspended or revoked by the Insurance Department, (c) terminated by the insurance company, or (d) otherwise terminated by law.

NOTE: In some States, Health Agents' licenses do not have to be renewed periodically, but remain in force perpetually until cancelled by one of the methods enumerated above.

Question 9:
If an Agent allows his license to be terminated, does he have to take a new examination in order to reinstate it?
Answer:
State rules vary. Nevertheless, basically, they are substantially as follows: If an applicant was required to pass a written State examination in order to obtain his original license, it is not necessary to take another State examination in order to have it reinstated. However, if an applicant had previously obtained a license without having previously passed a written State examination, he would not be able to secure the reinstatement of his license without first passing a written State examination if it had lapsed for more than a specified number of years.

Question 10:
On what grounds may a license be revoked?
Answer:
Usually, an Agent's license may be revoked or suspended because of:

a. A violation of the Insurance Law or any law while operating as an Agent.

b. A material misstatement in his application for a license.

c. Fraud or dishonesty.

INSURANCE LAW

d. Incompetence or untrustworthiness.

The suspension or revocation of an Agent's license terminates the authority of all Sub-licensees.

The Insurance Department may suspend or revoke a license (after a notice and a hearing) for any period of time which it feels is justified.

Question 11:
May a fine be levied instead of a revocation or suspension?
Answer:
In lieu of revocation or suspension of a license, the Insurance Department may require the payment of a fine, e.g., $500 for each violation up to five violations or a maximum penalty of $2,500. Usually, if the fine is unpaid within a stipulated period, the Insurance Department may revoke the license, or suspend it for such period as it may determine. However, generally the Insurance Department may not impose a revocation or suspension and a fine for the same offense.

Question 12:
Must an Agent maintain a separate bank account for the deposit of Premiums collected by him?
Answer:
An Agent acts in a fiduciary capacity for funds he collects, and may not mingle them with his own. However, he need not keep a separate bank account for each insurance company if he keeps records properly segregating the funds of each insurance company. He is permitted to deposit other funds in his Special Premium (Bank) Account for the following purposes: (a) to maintain an adequate bank balance, (b) to advance Return Premiums to his clients, and (c) to advance the payment of Premiums to the insurance company.

Question 13:
May an insurance company refer to its financial status in an advertisement?
Answer:
Yes. However, an insurance company may not advertise its financial condition without stating its assets, liabilities, legal reserves, and surplus to policyholders in accordance with the latest annual or quarterly statement. It may show assets and surplus (including capital stock) only as a notation on a circular or letter.

Question 14:
What information must be contained in an advertisement which refers to an insurance company?
Answer:
Every advertisement mentioning the name of an insurance company must state its full name, and the city, town, or village in the United States where it maintains its principal office.

INSURANCE LAW

Question 15:

a. State Insurance Laws prohibit "incomplete comparisons". What differences must an Agent take into account when making a comparison between two policies?

b. To what extent may an Agent assume the prospective Insured understands the provisions of both policies?

Answer:

a. A comparison is deemed incomplete if it does not take into account the following factors: (1) Gross Premiums; (2) dividends; (3) increases in cash values; (4) any other Benefits provided by the policy; (5) differences as to the length of time for which Premiums will be paid; (6) differences in limitations; and (7) differences in conditions or provisions which affect, directly or indirectly, the Benefits afforded under the policy.

b. The Agent must assume that the client knows nothing about either policy.

Question 16:

What is the status of statements made in the application?

Answer:

Statements in an application are representations and not warranties, and may not be changed without the applicant's written consent. The policy contains the entire contract except the rate schedules which are filed with the State Insurance Department. The application must be made a part of the policy to be admissible as evidence.

Question 17:

What is the significance of that part of State Insurance Laws which provides that statements of the applicant contained in a Health Insurance application are deemed representations and not warranties?

Answer:

A warranty is a statement which must be true literally, whereas a representation must only be substantially correct. Accordingly, a Health Insurance Company cannot void a policy, even within the Contestable Period (the first two years, or the first three years), for any trivial misstatements which the Insured may have made in his application for insurance provided that such statements were not material to the risk.

Question 18:

What is a material misrepresentation?

Answer:

The statements in an application for insurance are representations as to facts (past or present) made to an insurance company. An untrue statement or a false representation of a fact is a misrepresentation. An omission of a material fact can also be construed as a misrepresentation.

INSURANCE LAW

A statement (or a representation) is of a "material" nature if it is a factor which determines whether or not the policy is to be issued. Therefore, a material misrepresentation is a false statement (or material omission) of a past or present fact which, if the true facts were known to the insurance company, would have resulted in a refusal to issue the policy.

In an application for Health Insurance, every statement (or omission) which relates to conditions of health and previous medical attention and hospital care is deemed to be material to the risk, and a false statement or omission with respect to these facts is a material misrepresentation.

Question 19:
What is insurable interest?

Answer:
Any person of legal age may secure a policy covering himself as Insured and payable to anyone as Beneficiary. However, a person may not secure a policy on another person unless the Benefits are payable to the Insured or to a person having an *insurable interest* in the person insured.

An insurable interest exists in the following instances:

a. The interest engendered by the love and affection of persons closely related by blood or law.

b. An economic interest in the continued well-being and life of the Insured in the case of persons not included above.

A policy (except a Group Policy) may not be procured for another without his written application or consent. This requirement does not apply to a husband, wife, or minor children.

Question 20:
Usually, which provisions must be included in a Group Policy?

Answer:
Most States require the following provisions:

a. A statement made by the applicant, not contained in the signed application, may not void the insurance or reduce the Benefits. The application does not become a part of the policy as is the case in Individual Policies.

b. Statements in the application are deemed representations and not Warranties.

c. All new employees must be added to such Groups for which they are eligible.

d. Premiums must be remitted by the employer or, in the case of an association, by a designated person.

e. The insurance company must specify the conditions under which it will decline to renew.

INSURANCE LAW

f. Each insured member must receive an individual certificate summarizing the essential features of the coverage.

g. If there is an age limitation, it must be indicated in the policy.

h. Notice of sickness or injury must be given to the insurance company within 20 days. Failure to give notice within 20 days does not invalidate the claim if notice was given as soon as it was reasonably possible to do so.

i. The insurance company must furnish the policyholder with a blank Proof of Loss within 15 days after receipt of a Notice of Claim.

j. In case of claim, a written Proof of Loss must be furnished to the insurance company within 30 days, unless it is not reasonably possible to do so.

k. The insurance company has the right to examine the claimant as often as is reasonably necessary.

l. A loss should be paid within 60 days after receipt of a Proof of Loss unless the claim is made for loss of time, in which case the insurance company must remit payments at the end of each 30-day period.

m. The consent of the Beneficiary (except in the case of an Irrevocable Beneficiary) is not necessary in order to change the name of the Beneficiary, or for any other changes in the policy.

n. An action at law may not be instituted against the insurance company until at least 60 days after the filing of the Proof of Loss.

Question 21:
Does a Health Policy have to conform to State Law?

Answer:
Yes. A Health Policy may not be issued unless it meets the statutory requirements regarding *Required* and *Optional Provisions*. (Refer to the detailed explanations in the chapters pertaining to Required Uniform Policy Provisions and Optional Uniform Policy Provisions.)

Question 22:
What is Twisting?

Answer:
It is the making of misleading statements, misrepresentations, and/or incomplete comparisons to induce an Insured to drop present Health Insurance and replace it with other Health Insurance.

Question 23:
What is the penalty for Twisting?

Answer:
All States have severe penalties, such as the revocation of a license, criminal punishment consisting of a fine or imprisonment, or both, and a civil penalty in an amount equal to the commissions received.

INSURANCE LAW

Question 24:
What is Rebating? When is it allowed?

Answer:

Rebating is the paying, offering to pay or allow, the giving of anything of value, or any valuable consideration not specified in the policy to any person as an inducement to apply for and secure a policy of insurance.

Rebating is never allowed. It is a discrimination against those policyholders who do not receive a similar inducement to purchase their policies. Furthermore, it destroys the incentive of the Agent (or Broker) to perform his duties conscientiously, and it deprives the policyholder of competent and professional service. Generally, any person offering or accepting a rebate is subject to a penalty of as much as $500 for each such violation, in addition to all other penalties provided by law.

Question 25:
How is Group Health Insurance defined in the Insurance Law of most States?

Answer:

Usually, the Insurance Law contains the following definitions and restrictions:

a. Any policy written to cover one or more persons except a Blanket Accident Policy or an Individual Policy is considered a Group Policy.

b. All Group Policies must conform to the Insurance Law.

c. A policy issued to an employer (or to the trustees of a fund established by an employer) covering employees of such employer (for which the employer pays the Premium), must cover all of his employees, or all employees within a class(es) of employees.

d. Classes of employees are determined by conditions of employment.

e. If the Premiums are paid by funds contributed to by the employer and the employees, the contract must cover a stipulated percentage of the eligible employees.

f. A policy issued to the trustees of a fund (which was established by employers who are members of a trade association) for the sole benefit of the employees must conform to certain eligibility requirements.

g. A policy issued to the trustees of a fund established by two or more employers in the same industry, or one or more labor unions, or both, for the employees of the employers or members of the union must conform to certain minimum eligibility requirements.

h. Usually, the term "employees" is deemed to include employees of a single employer: officers, managers, employees, and retired employees of the employer and of subsidiary or affiliated corporations of a corporate employer, and the individual proprietors, partners, and (with

INSURANCE LAW

certain exceptions, e.g., a domestic) employees of individuals and firms of which the business is controlled by the insured employer.

i. Usually, the term "employers" includes any municipal corporation, any unincorporated municipality, or departments of such corporation or municipality determined by conditions pertaining to the employment.

j. Benefits are payable to the employee or other insured member of the group or Beneficiary designated by the employee other than the employer. Benefits for hospital, surgical, and medical expense may be assigned to the hospital or person(s) furnishing such aid.

k. Dependents of the employee may be included under Hospital, Surgical, and Medical Coverage.

l. The Insurance Department may require reasonable assumptions of morbidity or other appropriate claim rate, interest, and expenses of all insurance companies doing business in the State.

m. Each insurance company doing business in the State must file with the Insurance Department its schedule of Premium Rates, rules, and classifications of risks, and its maximum commissions, compensation, or other allowances to soliciting Agents (or Brokers). An insurance company may not issue a policy at a Premium Rate lower than those rates on file with the Insurance Department. Usually, this regulation applies only to the first year. Should the actual experience of any risk warrant it, a higher or lower rate may be charged.

n. The Insurance Department may adopt a Minimum Premium Rate for a Specific Group Coverage. This is done only after consulting with insurance companies writing this coverage(s). The Minimum Rate promulgated by the Insurance Department would apply to all insurance companies writing the coverage(s) in the State for the first policy year.

o. Any Group Policy may provide for a readjustment of the Premium Rate based on the actual experience of the Group at the end of the first year, and each year thereafter. Each adjustment must be limited to one year's experience. Refunds may be used to reduce the employer's contributions. If a refund exceeds the employer's contributions, that portion over the employer's contributions must be used only for the benefit of the employees.

Question 26:
How is a Blanket Accident and Health Policy defined in the Law?

Answer:
Usually, the Insurance Law contains the following definitions and restrictions:

A Blanket Accident and Health Policy is a contract of insurance issued against death or injury resulting from illness and/or accident which insures a group of persons conforming to one of the following requirements:

INSURANCE LAW

a. A policy may be issued to any railroad, steamship, motorbus, or airplane carrier of passengers. A "Group" is defined as all persons who may become such passengers, and protection may be afforded against death or bodily injury either while or as a result of being such passengers.

b. A policy may be issued to any employer to afford coverage for a group of employees who are exposed to exceptional hazards incident to such employment.

c. A policy may be issued to a school or to the authorities of the school covering the students or a group of students.

d. A policy may be issued in the name of any Volunteer Fire Department, having not less than 25 members and covering all members of the department.

e. A policy may be issued to an association of persons (incorporated or unincorporated) having a common interest or calling. The association must have at least 50 members and the policy must cover all members.

NOTE 1: All Benefits are paid to the person insured unless the insured person is a minor; in which event the Benefit is paid to the parent or person responsible for the support of the insured person.

NOTE 2: Usually, nothing contained in the Law is deemed to affect the legal liability of policyholders for the death or injury to any such members of the group.

Question 27:
What penalty is provided for persons who willfully circulate false statements or rumors regarding the financial condition of an insurance company?

Answer:
Usually, the violator is subject to a fine and/or imprisonment for willfully and knowingly circulating any such false statements or rumors.

Question 28:
What do State Laws usually provide with respect to false statements regarding the financial condition of firms or corporations (not insurance companies)?

Answer:
According to the laws of most States, it is a misdemeanor for any person willingly and knowingly to state, deliver, or transmit any false and untrue statement regarding the financial responsibility of any person, firm, or corporation with the intent that this untrue information should be acted upon.

Question 29:
What penalties are provided by State Insurance Laws to be imposed

INSURANCE LAW

upon any person who aids in the placing of insurance with insurance companies which are not authorized to transact business in the State?

Answer:

Usually, a fine is levied for the first offense, and additional fines may be levied thereafter if the Agent continues to violate the law, in addition to any other penalty provided by law, such as the suspension or revocation of licenses held by the violator.

Question 30:

Do State Insurance Laws regulate advertising which is done by an Agent?

Answer:

Yes. An Agent may not aid in the solicitation or negotiation of insurance for an unauthorized insurance company. An Agent who refers to an insurance company in an advertisement must set forth the name of the company in full, and must mention the name of the city, town, or village in which it has its principal office in the United States. An advertisement by an Agent must not contain any misrepresentations, misleading statements, or incomplete comparisons.

NOTE: If the advertisement shows the financial condition of an insurance company, it must comply with the law as explained previously.

Question 31:

A client wishes to buy insurance from an insurance company not licensed in his State. May a person licensed as an Agent in his State handle the transaction?

Answer:

No. It is a violation of the Insurance Law to act as an Agent for an insurance company which is not licensed in the State, i.e., an unauthorized insurance company.

Question 32:

A person offers to introduce you to his friends in order to enable you to sell insurance to them provided that you will pay him part of your commissions. May this be done?

Answer:

No, not unless such person is licensed as an Agent representing the insurance company with which the insurance is to be placed.

Question 33:

A client asks your advice with regard to his ordering an insurance policy by mail from an insurance company not licensed in your State. The company advertises low rates and good service. What should you advise him?

INSURANCE LAW

Answer:

The client should be advised that he would be better off if he did not purchase insurance from an unauthorized insurance company. One of the reasons the company is not licensed could be that its financial condition does not meet with the minimum requirements of the State Laws. Furthermore, it may have a very limited policy or a poor record for paying valid claims.

In addition, if a claim arose which was disputed or denied by the insurance company, the policyholder could not obtain the same assistance from his State Insurance Department in connection with such a claim as is available in connection with authorized insurance companies.

In some States, it is possible to sue an unauthorized insurance company in the State in which the policy was issued. Still, it may be difficult to collect any judgment obtained if the insurance company does not maintain funds in such State. Suit would have to be brought in some other State on the judgment obtained in the client's State. This could cause much inconvenience and hardship to the policyholder or his Beneficiary.

If the client still insists upon doing business with an unauthorized insurance company, the Agent should refuse to aid him, because it is a violation of State Insurance Laws for an Agent to assist, in any way, in the placing of insurance with an insurance company that is not authorized to transact business in the client's State.

Question 34:

What are the Agent's (or Broker's) obligations to the Insurance Department?

Answer:

In addition to adhering to the regulations of the Insurance Department, the Agent (or Broker) should assist the Insurance Department in the enforcement of these regulations. He should report to the Insurance Department all violations of which he is aware.

Question 35:

What are the obligations of an Agent (or Broker) to his insurance company?

Answer:

The Agent (or Broker) is required to supply his insurance company with all necessary underwriting information, transmit promptly money due the insurance company, and represent the insurance company in a courteous, efficient, and honest manner.

Question 36:

What are the responsibilities of an Agent (or Broker) to other insurance companies and Agents (or Brokers) in competition with him?

INSURANCE LAW

Answer:
The Agent (or Broker) should treat them honestly and fairly.

Question 37:
What are the responsibilities of an Agent (or Broker) to his policyholders?

Answer:
The Agent (or Broker) should analyze his policyholder's needs honestly and make his recommendations based on the requirements and the circumstances of the policyholder.

Question 38:
What are the responsibilities of the Agent (or Broker) to the insurance industry and to the public?

Answer:
The Agent (or Broker) should keep abreast of the changes in the field of Health Insurance and should consider his position as one of public trust. His actions and practices should be such as would bring credit to himself and the insurance industry as a whole.

Question 39:
What do the State Insurance Laws provide with respect to unfair or deceptive acts or practices?

Answer:
Generally, the Laws prohibit any unfair method of competition or any unfair or deceptive acts or practices in the insurance business. Usually, it is a misdemeanor to engage in any such acts.

REVIEW QUESTIONS

Question 1:
Why would one clerk be rated "A" and another rated "D" even though they are the same age?

Answer:
The duties of their occupations may be different. For example, one may be a clerk in a bank, whereas the other may be a clerk on a construction job.

Question 2:
With respect to an airplane accident, would the Insured be covered under a Disability Income Policy if he were:
 a. Hit by a propeller?
 b. Injured while stranded in a life boat?
 c. Hurt while boarding a plane?

Answer:
 a. Yes.
 b. Yes.
 c. Yes.

Question 3:
Would a claim be denied (within the contestable period) under the following circumstances:
 a. Misstatement on the application regarding the occupation of the Insured?
 b. Failure to reveal a prior disability on the application?

Answer:
 a. No, except in those rare instances where the occupation was so hazardous that it was uninsurable.
 b. Yes, if it were serious and would have rendered the person uninsurable.

Question 4:
Explain what is meant by Elective Indemnity.

Answer:
If, as the result of an accident, a person suffers a dislocation, fracture, or loss of fingers or toes, he may elect to accept a lump sum payment in lieu of Monthly (or Weekly) Benefits. The amount of the lump sum payment is determined in accordance with a schedule appearing in the policy.

Question 5:
With respect to the Monthly (or Weekly) Indemnity Coverage under a Cancellable Disability Income Policy, which answer is the most correct?
 It should be:

REVIEW QUESTIONS

    a. Enough to cover all lost income and any extra expense not otherwise compensated.

    b. Not more than 75% of total income.

    c. As much Premium as the Insured can afford to pay.

    d. Not more than 75% of earned income.

Answer:
    Part "d" is most correct.

Question 6:
How would you explain the following:
    a. Insuring Agreement?
    b. Probationary Period?
    c. Commercial Policy?

Answer:
    a. The Insuring Agreement defines the scope of the coverage.

    b. The Probationary Period is the period of time between the effective date of the policy and the date the *Sickness Coverage* becomes effective.

    c. A Commercial Policy is written to cover a person in a *less hazardous occupation*. It is virtually free of restrictions. It has high limits and Benefits are available for long periods. Premiums are payable annually, semiannually, or quarterly.

Question 7:
For which of the following is the Principal Sum payable? Loss of:
    a. Both hands.
    b. One hand and one foot.
    c. Thumb and index finger.
    d. Both feet.
    e. One eye and one hand.
    f. Accidental death.

Answer:
    Accidental death.

Question 8:
    Under which circumstances are Total Disability payments made: (a) The Insured is unable to perform an important duty pertaining to his occupation? (b) The Insured is unable to perform any work for remuneration?

Answer:
    The definition of Total Disability is not uniform. Depending upon the insurance company and on the policy, payments may be made under either circumstances.

REVIEW QUESTIONS

Question 9:
What is the correct number of days that should be inserted in the following blank spaces:

a. A Notice of Sickness must be given to the insurance company within .... days.

b. A Notice of Accident must be given to the insurance company within .... days.

c. The insurance company must furnish a blank Proof of Loss within .... days.

d. A Proof of Loss must be furnished to the insurance company within .... days after the date of the loss.

Answer:
- a. 20 days.
- b. 20 days.
- c. 15 days.
- d. 90 days.

Question 10:
What is meant by a Guaranteed Renewable Policy?

Answer:
The insurance company may not cancel or refuse to renew the policy as long as the Insured pays his Premiums.

However, the insurance company has the right to increase the Premium on the anniversary date, but such increase in the Premium must apply to all policies in the same class.

Question 11:
What is the difference between a Guaranteed Renewable Policy and a Noncancellable and Guaranteed Renewable Policy?

Answer:
In both cases, the insurance company must renew the policy as long as the Insured continues to pay his Premium. The insurance company may raise the rates of a Guaranteed Renewable Policy on a class basis, but may not increase the rate of a Noncancellable and Guaranteed Renewable Policy.

Question 12:
a. Under Group Coverage, explain what is meant by Contributory Plan.

b. Does a Group Policy generally contain a provision for the conversion of the coverage if an employee leaves an employer?

c. What Benefits are generally provided under a Group Policy?

REVIEW QUESTIONS

Answer:

a. The cost is shared by both the employer and employee.

b. Yes.

c. Accidental Death and Dismemberment Benefits; Sickness and Accident Weekly Income Benefit; Hospital Expense Benefit; Surgical Expense Benefit; Medical Expense Benefit; Major Medical Expense Benefit; and Blanket Accident Benefit.

Question 13:

In an Individual Health Policy, would the Insured be covered under the following conditions? Explain.

a. An Insured purchased a policy, while employed as a clerk in an office. He changed his occupation without notifying the insurance company. He is injured while engaged in his new occupation as a tractor operator on a construction job.

b. When the Insured applied for a policy, he did not mention any history of a serious illness suffered during the five years prior thereto. Subsequently, and before the Time Limit on Certain Defenses had expired, he sustained a disabling injury, and the insurance company learned that two years prior to the date of application he had been treated for an internal cancer.

c. On his application, an Insured indicated that he was 40 years of age. Following a disabling injury, it was learned that he was 45 years of age at the time that he had applied for coverage.

Answer:

a. If the Change of Occupation Optional Uniform Provision is not incorporated in the policy, the Insured is covered for the full amount of Benefits. However, if the policy contains this provision, the insurance company would not be obligated to pay more than that portion of indemnity which the Premium paid would have purchased at the rates and within the limits applicable to the more hazardous occupation (in accordance with the insurance company's filings and regulations).

b. No. The prior existence of internal cancer would have made the applicant uninsurable. He deliberately withheld information which would have made him unacceptable to the underwriter.

NOTE 1: If a policy contained a Two-Year Incontestable Clause, the insurance company would be prevented from denying liability after two years from the effective date of the policy, except if the clause contained the phrase "except for fraudulent misstatements" or in the case of proven fraud.

NOTE 2: If the Insured were not aware of the existence of cancer (sometimes a doctor may not inform his patient), the Insured would not be guilty of a misrepresentation.

c. Yes, but the Benefits would be reduced proportionately, i.e., based upon the amount of insurance that the Premium paid would have purchased at the correct age.

REVIEW QUESTIONS

Question 14:
An Insured permits a Health Policy to lapse. Upon payment of the Premium, the insurance company reinstates the policy. Four days after the reinstatement of his policy, he is striken with a serious illness. Is he covered? Explain.

Answer:
If the policy does not cover a loss resulting from sickness until 10 days after the payment and acceptance of the Reinstatement Premium, coverage would not be afforded for that illness. If the policy covers a loss resulting from sickness commencing on or after the date of reinstatement, the Insured would be covered for that illness.

Question 15:
An Insured permits a Health Policy to lapse. Upon the payment of his Premium, the insurance company reinstates the policy. The day after reinstatement, he is killed in an accident. Is he covered? Explain.

Answer:
Yes. The Reinstatement Provision provides that the Accident Benefit Coverage becomes effective immediately.

Question 16:
a. What is meant by Double Indemnity? Cite at least two circumstances under which it is paid.

b. An Insured carries a Health Policy providing $250 Monthly Indemnity, 50 months Death, Dismemberment, and Loss of Sight Benefits, and Blanket Medical Expense. He is involved in an accident in which he loses both feet. He is totally disabled for one month, and incurs medical expenses of $960. If, because of the type of accident, the insurance company were required to pay Double Indemnity, how much would he receive under each Benefit?

Answer:
a. Double Indemnity provides for double the normal Benefits if the loss is sustained under certain special circumstances described in the policy. For example, an injury may be sustained while the policyholder is a passenger on a common carrier (not aircraft); or he may be injured by the explosion of a steam boiler. (Note: The Medical Expense Benefit is not doubled.)

b. $25,000 (Capital Sum) for dismemberment and loss of sight (50 months doubled). $500 monthly income for one month ($250 doubled). $960 medical expense (not doubled).

NOTE: Most insurance companies pay the Monthly Benefit due prior to the actual dismemberment or loss of sight.

Question 17:
In each of the following, explain your answer:

REVIEW QUESTIONS

a. An Insured is involved in an accident in which he loses all of his fingers of his right hand. Would he be paid under the Dismemberment Benefit of a Health Policy?

b. An Insured loses the sight of both eyes for six weeks as the result of an accident. What would he be paid under the Loss of Sight Benefit?

Answer:

a. Although most policies provide a Benefit for the loss of a hand, this would not be considered the loss of a hand (refer to the definition of dismemberment). Some policies provide for the loss of fingers and toes under dismemberment, in which case a Benefit would be paid thereunder.

b. Nothing. In order to collect a Loss of Sight Benefit, the loss of sight must be complete, total, and irrecoverable.

Question 18:

a. With respect to Personal Sickness Coverage what is meant by the Elimination Period and what effect does it have on the Premium?

b. An Insured has a policy affording $300 Monthly Indemnity with a 7-day Elimination Period. He is Totally Disabled due to illness for 49 days. How much Monthly Indemnity will be receive? Explain.

Answer:

a. An Elimination Period is the period of time between the date of disability to the date a Benefit begins to accrue. The longer the Elimination Period, the lower the Premium.

b. $420. He was disabled for 49 days, and he is not paid for the first 7 days; 1.4 months (42 days) times $300 equals $420.

Question 19:

a. With respect to Personal Accident Coverage, what factors determine the rate to be charged?

b. With respect to Personal Health Insurance, what is the moral hazard of a risk, and why is it important?

Answer:

a. The Benefits, age, occupation, and sex of the Insured determine the rate.

NOTE: Insurance companies that write Rated (Substandard) Risks also consider the physical condition in determining the rate.

b. The habits, ethics, and financial background of the Insured determine the moral hazard. As in the case of a poor physical history, a poor moral risk increases the possibility of claims, and increases the probability of a longer duration of each claim.

Question 20:

Under a Family Hospital and Surgical Policy, does a dependent child have the right to demand that a policy be issued in his name when he reaches 19 years of age, and is no longer covered by a Family Policy?

REVIEW QUESTIONS

Answer:
Yes, provided that he applies for it within 30 days after his 19th birthday. The insurance company must issue a policy for him, regardless of his physical condition at that time. (Some insurance companies afford coverage for an unmarried dependent child until age 23.)

Question 21:
If an error is made on an application for an Individual Health Policy, how may the error be corrected?

Answer:
A new application may be completed, or the Insured may write a letter, a copy of which is attached to the policy. Most insurance companies allow the applicant to initial the changes in the application.

Question 22:
If an Insured is injured in an accident, and is unable to notify the insurance company within 20 days, but notifies the company as soon as he is able to do so, is he entitled to Benefits? Explain.

Answer:
Yes. The Insured has complied with the requirements of the policy if he notifies the insurance company of the injury as soon as he is able to do so.

Question 23:
Which type of coverage would you recommend to a businessman, but not to a student?

Answer:
Disability Income Coverage.

Question 24:
During the day, a man works as a draftsman; but during the evening, he works as a chauffeur. Which classification would apply?

Answer:
The classification of chauffeur would apply since it is more hazardous.

Question 25:
Explain:
a. Policy Fee.
b. Grace Period.
c. Rated (Substandard) Risk.

Answer:
a. The first Premium is increased by a small charge (e.g., $5). This is known as a Policy Fee. Some insurance companies pay it (or part of it) to the Agent as a portion of his commission.

REVIEW QUESTIONS

b. A Grace Period is the period of time following the date upon which a Premium was due, during which coverage is continued.

c. An applicant who does not qualify for a Standard Policy may be insured under a Rated (Substandard) Policy, usually at a higher rate.

Question 26:
What benefit is derived by a community as a result of the fact that a person carries an Individual Health Policy?

Answer:
It relieves the community of the burden of providing free medical care for the disabled person, and the necessities of life for his family.

Question 27:
What is overinsurance and how can it be prevented?

Answer:
Overinsurance exists if: (a) Income Benefits payable for disability exceed the normal earned income, and/or (b) the Medical Expense Benefit is greater than the regular charges made by hospitals, doctors, or for other therapeutic services or supplies.

Insurance companies avoid the first situation by limiting the Benefits payable to a percentage of the Insured's earned income; and the latter situation by limiting the amount of coverage to reasonable limits.

In both of the above instances, the temptation to malinger is eliminated by utilizing a Nonduplication of Benefits Provision (i.e., the Relations of Earnings to Insurance Provision, Other Insurance in This Insurer Provision, or Insurance with Other Insurers Provision).

Question 28:
Explain the difference between a Commercial Health Policy and an Industrial Health Policy with respect to:

a. Coverage.

b. Method of Premium payment.

Answer:
a. A Commercial Policy has higher limits and longer Benefit Periods.

b. The Premium for a Commercial Policy is payable quarterly, semi-annually, or annually. The Premium for an Industrial Policy is payable weekly or monthly.

Question 29:
On May 10th, two persons received Disability Income Policies, each of which provided a Benefit of $200 per month. Each policy had a 14-day Elimination Period for accident and sickness and a 14-day Probationary Period. Would there be coverage in the following cases?

a. On May 12th, A suffered an accident which left him Totally Disabled for 44 days.

REVIEW QUESTIONS

b. *On May 18th, B contracted pneumonia and was disabled for five weeks.*

Answer:

a. He would collect $200; 44 days minus 14 days (Elimination Period) equals one month at $200 per month, payable as an Accident Benefit.

b. No coverage. The Insured became ill during the Probationary Period. A sickness contracted during a Probationary Period is not covered.

Question 30:

A prospective client says he does not need Heatlh Insurance because his employer pays his salary while he is ill. How might you convince him that he does need such protection?

Answer:

He will need additional funds with which to pay his medical bills and other increased expenses. Furthermore, he probably does not have a guarantee that the employer will continue to pay his salary for *an unlimited period of time.*

If his employer has agreed to continue his salary for a specified period (e.g., 3 or 6 months), the Elimination Period of the employee's Health Policy should be (but is not compulsory) the same as the salary continuance period. The longer the Elimination Period, the lower the Premium.

Question 31:

Mr. A had a Health Policy which was cancelled for nonpayment of Premium on November 4. On November 10, he reported an accident to the insurance company which had occurred on November 1. Would he be covered for expenses for that accident?

Answer:

Yes. The accident occurred prior to the effective date of cancellation.

Question 32:

May a person collect under both a Workers' Compensation Policy and a Health Policy for the same injury?

Answer:

Yes. Unless the policy specifically excludes coverage if protection is afforded under Workers' Compensation Insurance. Some Hospitalization Policies contain such an exclusion, whereas, most Individual Income Policies do not.

Question 33:

For which forms of Health Insurance Coverage would a retired man be eligible?

Answer:

Accidental Death, Dismemberment, Loss of Sight, and all of the various coverages for medical expenses.

REVIEW QUESTIONS

Question 34:
May the insurance company demand an autopsy in the event of accidental death?
Answer:
Yes, if not prohibited by Law.

Question 35:
A man has an Accident Policy with insurance company A providing $150 Monthly Indemnity, and a similar policy with insurance company B. Both policies require prorating in the event of the existence of other insurance that had not been described in the application. When the Insured became Totally Disabled, each insurance company discovered the existence of the other policy. How much does each insurance company pay?
Answer:
$75 per month.

Question 36:
The Insured has a Health Policy which provides $300 Monthly Benefits. The policy stipulates that if the Insured obtains other policies with other insurance companies, he is required to notify the first insurance company. The Insured took out a Health Policy with another insurance company which provided $600 Monthly Benefits, but did not notify the first insurance company. If the Insured suffered a disability, what would the first insurance company be required to pay:

a. $300 per month?
b. $150 per month?
c. $100 per month?

Answer:
$100 per month.

NOTE: This figure is obtained by prorating the Benefit. The total insurance in force was $900 per month. The first insurance company had agreed to pay a Benefit of $300 per month, which represented ⅓ of the aggregate coverage. Accordingly, the first insurance company pays ⅓ of its agreed amount of $300 per month, which is $100 per month (⅓ × $300 = $100). The excess Premiums are returned.

Question 37:
A policy affords $500 Blanket Medical Coverage.

a. Which of the following expenses would be covered: Surgical, Medication, Braces, Registered Nurses, and Physicians?

b. How much will be paid if one loss amounts to $575 and another amounts to $450?

Answer:
a. All, up to the $500 limit.

REVIEW QUESTIONS

b. The insurance company will pay for all the aforementioned expenses up to a maximum of $500 for each loss. Accordingly, the Insured will receive $500 for the first loss and $450 for the second loss.

Question 38:
An applicant earns $500 a month. He has a policy with an insurance company providing for Monthly Disability Benefits of $100. Would you be able to write an additional policy in another insurance company providing Monthly Disability Benefits of $200?

Answer:
Yes. Generally, protection may be obtained in the aggregate up to 75% or 80% of earned income. However, some insurance companies take into consideration a predetermined amount for Social Security Benefits in order to ascertain the appropriate insurable percentage.

NOTE: Since the Monthly Disability Benefit payments are not taxable, many insurance companies limit the protection to approximately 50% of the Insured's earned income.

Question 39:
What should an Insured do if an insurance company does not send a blank Proof of Loss to him?

Answer:
Write a letter giving the details of the loss and the manner in which it was sustained.

Question 40:
Does the insurance company have a right to make a physical examination of the Insured if he presents a claim?

Answer:
Yes, as frequently as reasonably required.

Question 41:
If, after the Insured has read the policy, he decides it is not what he desires, may he return it and receive a full refund of his Premium?

Answer:
Yes, if he returns it within 10 days after having received it. This would not apply to Short Term Single Premium Policies (e.g., Aviation Accident Policies).

Question 42:
If an Insured purchased Double Indemnity Coverage on his Health Policy, would he be protected for Double Indemnity under the following circumstances? Answer yes or no.

a. While the Insured was a passenger on a freight elevator, it dropped two floors causing injuries to the Insured.

REVIEW QUESTIONS

b. *An Insured, who was a passerby, ran into a burning building to save a child. The Insured was injured while inside the building.*

c. *The Insured was injured while driving his friend's automobile.*

d. *The Insured was injured while riding as a passenger in a railroad train.*

Answer:

a. No.
b. No.
c. No.
d. Yes.

Question 43:
Some of the following statements in connection with Commercial and Industrial types of Health Insurance are true whereas some are false. If a statement is false, correct it.

a. *An Industrial Health Policy covers all employees working for a common employer.*

b. *A Commercial Policy is subject to fewer restrictions than an Industrial Policy.*

c. *The limits of a Commercial Policy are lower than the limits of an Industrial Policy.*

Answer:

a. False. A Group Policy covers all employees working for a common employer.

b. True.

c. False. The limits of a Commercial Policy are higher than the limits of an Industrial Policy.

Question 44:
In Group Insurance, what factors determine:

a. *The rate?*

b. *The gross cost?*

c. *The net cost?*

Answer:

a. The age, occupation, and sex of the employees and the type of Benefits offered.

b. The rate times the exposure (number of persons to be covered).

c. The losses of the Group and the expenses incurred by the insurance company.

Question 45:
Under a Major Medical Policy, how do the following affect a claim?

a. *A $500 Deductible Clause.*

b. *A 75%-25% Coinsurance Provision (Insured Percentage).*

REVIEW QUESTIONS

c. *A $5,000 maximum.*

d. *A Two-Year Time Limit Provision.*

Answer:
 a. The insurance company is not liable for the first $500 of eligible expenses.

 b. The insurance company will pay 75% of the covered expenses, and the Insured must pay 25% of the covered expenses.

 c. Generally, the insurance company's Maximum Limit of Liability is $5,000 for each injury or illness for each insured person.

 d. The insurance company's liability is limited to the expense incurred during the first two years following the date of the commencement of the disability.

Question 46:
 a. *What factors may an employer use in determining the classifications of employees for a Group Insurance Program?*

 b. *What percentage of eligible employees must participate in the program?*

Answer:
 a. The following factors may be used in determining the classifications based on the condition of employment: wages, job titles, locations, length of service, etc.

 b. If the program is noncontributory, 100%. If the program is contributory, 75%.

Question 47:
 Under a Family Hospitalization Policy, explain the following Benefits:

 a. *Room and Board.*

 b. *Miscellaneous Hospital.*

 c. *First Aid.*

Answer:
 a. The Room and Board Benefit is the dollar amount of coverage afforded by the policy for the payment of the hospital room and board charges.

 b. The Miscellaneous Hospital Benefit is the dollar Benefit for which protection is afforded under the policy for the payment of the hospital's charges for drugs, dressings, X-rays, etc.

 c. The First Aid Benefit is the dollar Benefit for which protection is afforded under the policy for the payment of charges made by a hospital for first aid treatment required because of an accident.

REVIEW QUESTIONS

Question 48:
Does the surgery have to be performed in the hospital in order for an Insured to be eligible for the Surgical Expense Benefit?

Answer:
No.

Question 49:
Is the Hospitalization Coverage limited to certain hospitals?

Answer:
No. Most policies pay the Benefit if the Insured is confined to any licensed hospital in the world provided that an out-of-pocket loss had been incurred.

Question 50:
Are the Benefits paid to the Insured or to the hospital?

Answer:
Most policies pay the Benefits to the Insured unless he authorizes the insurance company to pay the hospital.

GLOSSARY OF HEALTH INSURANCE TERMS

The following definitions are in common use and are acceptable to practically all insurance companies that issue Health Insurance Policies. However, some insurance companies may interpret these terms differently. Therefore, it is not advisable to infer that they are subject to merely one interpretation. A careful reading of these terms will simplify your analysis of the Multiple Choice questions which appear on the examinations conducted by many State supervisory bodies.

ACCIDENT — an unforeseen, unintended, unexpected event, mishap, or casualty.

ACCIDENTAL BODILY INJURY — bodily injury resulting from an accident.

ACCIDENTAL BODILY INJURY CLAUSE — Insuring Clause which requires only that accidental bodily injury be sustained, regardless of the cause. More liberal than the Accidental Means Clause.

ACCIDENTAL DEATH, DISMEMBERMENT, AND LOSS OF SIGHT BENEFIT — a form of insurance affording Benefits in the event of accidental death, accidental loss of a member(s), e.g., an arm or a leg, or the accidental loss of sight.

ACCIDENTAL DEATH BENEFIT — a lump sum payment for loss of life due to an accident which was the direct cause of death. The cause of the mishap must be accidental in order for a Benefit to be payable.

ACCIDENTAL MEANS — an unforeseen, unexpected, unintended cause of an accident which results in an injury.

ACCIDENTAL MEANS CLAUSE — Insuring Clause which covers only those injuries caused by an accident which was unintended, unexpected, and unforeseen. The cause must be accidental.

ACCUMULATION PROVISION — a percentage increase of the Benefits available under the policy, intended as a bonus to the Insured for continuous renewals. (Usually, it is not included in policies issued currently.)

ACQUISITION COST — the immediate cost of issuing a new policy. It includes medical and inspection fees, commissions, clerical costs, etc.

ACTUARY — a person who calculates policy rates, reserves, and dividends and prepares various other applicable statistical studies and reports.

ADDITIONAL RESERVE FOR NONCANCELLABLE POLICIES — refer to Policy Reserve.

ADJUSTABLE PREMIUM — the agreed right of an insurance company to modify the Insured's Premium payments under certain specified conditions. Usually, this provision is contained in Cancellable Policies. Some Noncancellable Policies have a step-up-rate which increases at a specified age and at a specified rate.

ADVERSE SELECTION — the tendency of more poor risks than good ones to buy insurance or maintain existing insurance in force, i.e., selection against the insurance company.

GLOSSARY OF HEALTH INSURANCE TERMS

AGE LIMITS — minimum or maximum age limits for the insuring of new applicants or for the renewal of policies.

AGENT — an insurance company representative, licensed by the State, who solicits insurance for the insurance company(ies) for which he is licensed.

AGENT, GENERAL — a General Agent (comparable to a Manager of an agency) who is given supervisory authority over the Agents under his jurisdiction. Usually, he performs the following functions: selecting, writing, and servicing the business in force in his territory. Generally, he signs contracts with Agents to sell and service the insurance companies' policies. Usually, a General Agent is not an employee of the Health Insurance Company.

AGGREGATE AMOUNT — the maximum dollar amount that can be collected under any policy, for any disability or period of disability.

ALLOCATED BENEFITS — payments (in some policies) for specified hospital services (X-rays, drugs, dressings, etc.) which are limited to maximum specified amounts.

APPLICATION — a form containing a series of questions eliciting pertinent information, e.g., name, address, earnings, insurance and medical history, etc. The applicant must sign the application which serves as a basis for underwriting the risk and which becomes a part of the policy.

ASSIGNEE — a person, firm, or corporation to whom the rights under a policy are assigned in their entirety or in part.

ASSIGNMENT — the signed transfer of the Benefits of a policy by an Insured to a third party.

ASSOCIATION GROUP — Individual Policies written to cover members of a trade or professional association.

AVERAGE EARNINGS CLAUSE — a provision in the policy which permits the insurance company to reduce the Monthly Income Disability Benefits payable if the Insured's Total Income Benefits exceed either his current monthly earnings or his average monthly earnings during the two-year period immediately preceding the disability. However, the operation of this provision may not reduce the total of all Benefits to the Insured below $200 per month. This applies only to Guaranteed Renewable Policies and Noncancellable and Guaranteed Renewable Policies.

AVIATION TRIP INSURANCE — a policy covering an individual as a passenger of a scheduled aircraft. Generally, it is purchased at the airport.

BENEFICIARY — a person(s) designated to receive a specified cash payment in the event of the policyholder's death due to an accident.

BENEFICIARY, CONTINGENT (SECONDARY) — a person who is entitled to Benefits only after the death of a Primary Beneficiary.

BENEFICIARY IRREVOCABLE — the Insured may not change the designated Beneficiary without the Beneficiary's consent.

GLOSSARY OF HEALTH INSURANCE TERMS

BENEFICIARY, PRIMARY — a person who is entitled primarily to Benefits upon the death of an Insured.

BENEFICIARY, REVOCABLE — the designated Beneficiary may be changed at the Insured's request without the consent of the Beneficiary.

BINDING RECEIPT — refer to Conditional Receipt.

BLANKET ACCIDENT MEDICAL EXPENSE — entitles the Insured who suffered a bodily injury to collect up to a maximum established in the policy for all hospital and medical expense incurred, without any limitations on individual types of medical expenses.

BLANKET POLICY — covers a number of individuals who are exposed to the same hazards such as members of an athletic team who are passengers in the same plane.

BLUE CROSS — an independent, nonprofit membership association providing protection against the costs of hospital care in a limited geographical area.

BLUE SHIELD — an independent, nonprofit membership association providing protection against the costs of surgery and other items of medical care in a limited geographical area.

BROKER — an insurance solicitor, licensed by the State, who represents various Insureds, and who is permitted to place General Insurance Coverages with any insurance company authorized to transact business in the State in which he is licensed.

BUSINESS INSURANCE — a policy which provides Benefits for a business rather than for an individual. It indemnifies for the loss of services of a key employee or a partner who becomes disabled.

CANCELLABLE POLICY — a policy which may be terminated either by the Insured or the insurance company by notification to the other party in accordance with the terms of the policy.

CAPITAL SUM — the amount payable for accidental loss of two members or both eyes (or one of each). An Indemnity for the loss of one member or the sight of one eye is usually a percentage of the Capital Sum. Under Income Protection Policies, usually, the maximum Capital Sum is 200 times the Weekly Income Benefit or 50 times the Monthly Benefit.

CATASTROPHE INSURANCE — refer to Major Medical Expense Insurance.

CERTIFICATE OF INSURANCE — each person who is covered by a Group Insurance Policy receives a Certificate. The Certificate indicates the Benefits to which the Insured is entitled and the pertinent conditions of the Master Contract.

CLAIM — a demand to the insurance company for the payment of Benefits under a policy.

CLAIM RATIO — the ratio for claims or losses to Earned Premium.

CLAIM RESERVES — the liability of the insurance company for an event which has not yet occurred (often called Loss Reserves).

GLOSSARY OF HEALTH INSURANCE TERMS

CLASSIFICATION — the underwriting occupational category into which a risk is placed depending upon his susceptibility to injury or illness.

CLASSIFICATION MANUAL — a manual pertaining to the occupational classification system used by insurance companies.

CLASSIFIED INSURANCE (SUBSTANDARD INSURANCE) — insurance offered to an applicant who has some form of physical impairment, unfavorable family or personal history or environment, hazardous occupation, etc. The Premium is higher in order to provide for the greater risk involved.

COINSURANCE (INSURED PERCENTAGE) — a provision which specifies that the insurance company will pay only part of a loss and requires the policyholder to pay the balance himself. For example, in the case of Major Medical Expense Insurance, the insurance company may be obliged to pay 75% of an Insured's expenses in excess of the Deductible Amount, if any, and the Insured is required to pay the other 25% himself.

COMMERCIAL POLICY — a policy in which the insurance company retains the right to cancel or refuse to renew the coverage. The Premiums are payable quarterly, semiannually, or annually.

COMMISSIONS — payments made by an insurance company to the Agent for the sale and servicing of a policy. Commissions are calculated as a specific percentage of the Premium paid and the percentage is determined in accordance with the contract between the Agent and his insurance company. Some insurers charge an initial policy fee which is sometimes given to the Agent to supplement his regular first commission.

COMMON CARRIER — an individual or concern engaged in the transportation of goods or persons in return for a fee, based upon uniform rates to all persons.

COMPREHENSIVE MAJOR MEDICAL INSURANCE — a policy designed to give the protection offered by both a Basic and a Major Medical Policy. It is characterized by a low Deductible Amount, Coinsurance Clause, and High Maximum Benefits, e.g., $50,000. This policy is generally referred to by the shortened term of "Comprehensive Insurance".

COMPULSORY DISABILITY INSURANCE — refer to Statutory Disability Benefits Law.

CONDITIONAL RECEIPT — a receipt given for the payment of the first Premium (accompanying the application) which binds the insurance company on the contract if the risk is approved as applied for, subject to the other conditions set forth in the receipt.

CONFINING SICKNESS — requires confinement of the Insured at home, in a hospital, or in a sanitarium in order to be entitled to collect for Income Benefits.

GLOSSARY OF HEALTH INSURANCE TERMS

Consideration — one of the elements of a binding contract. The Premium payment and the statements made by the prospective Insured in the application are construed as the Insured's consideration. The insurance company's acceptance of the Premium and its promise to pay are construed as its consideration.

Consideration Clause — the Uniform Policy Provisions Law requires that the policy indicate the entire amount of money or any other consideration therefor.

Contingency Reserves — voluntary reserves which represent portions of surplus other than true liability maintained for exceptional emergencies. The number and severity of Health Insurance claims vary with the seasons of the year. Furthermore, there is always a possibility that catastrophic losses (e.g., epidemics) may require an unexpected number of claim payments.

Continuous Disability — disability that is unbroken or uninterrupted by a recovery of good health or by a return to work.

Contributory Group Plans — plans under which the members of the Group pay a part of the Premium.

Conversion Privilege — the right granted the Insured to change his protection from a Group Policy to an Individual Policy upon termination of his Group Coverage. He is given an opportunity to secure an Individual Policy within a specified period thereafter regardless of whether or not he is in good health at that time.

Coordinated Benefits (Nonduplication of Benefits Provision) — a provision according to which the Benefits afforded under another policy are considered and coordinated with the Benefits of the policy involved so that double or duplicated Benefits are not paid under two or more separate policies. Generally, the inclusion of this provision results in a lower Premium.

Corridor Deductible — the amount that must be paid by the Insured over and above the amount payable under the policy for basic Hospital and Medical Benefits before Major Medical Expense Benefits become effective.

Deductible — the amount of loss or expense that must be incurred by the Insured before Benefits become payable. The insurance company pays Benefits only for the loss in excess of the amount specified in the Deductible Provision. There are various types of Deductible Provisions.

Disability — a physical condition which makes an Insured incapable of performing one or more duties of his occupation, or, in the case of Total Disability, prevents him from performing any other type of work for remuneration. (This wording varies from one insurance company to another.)

GLOSSARY OF HEALTH INSURANCE TERMS

DISABILITY INCOME INSURANCE — a form of Health Insurance that provides periodic payments to replace income while the Insured is unable to work as a result of an injury, illness, or disease.

DISCLOSURE STATEMENT — a form required in some States which must be given to an applicant for a Health Policy. It contains a brief summary of the Benefits afforded and reductions or limitations of the policy in a manner which discourages the misrepresentation of the actual coverage afforded thereunder. The statement must be given to the applicant at the time the application is made or it must be delivered with the policy. An acknowledgment of the receipt of this form must be furnished to the insurer by the applicant.

DISMEMBERMENT — loss of a hand or foot by severance through or above the wrist or ankle joints.

DIVIDEND — a refund of part of the Premium under a Participating Policy; a share of policyholder surplus funds apportioned for distribution. They are derived from savings in mortality, expenses, and interest earned in excess of the assumed rate used in the calculation of the Premiums and the Reserves.

DOUBLE INDEMNITY — a clause providing for the payment of twice the regular Benefit if an injury is sustained under certain specified circumstances. This is a more limited Benefit than a Double Indemnity Benefit under Life Insurance Policies.

DUPLICATE COVERAGE — a term usually applied to Benefits (other than loss of time) where an Insured is covered by several policies with one or more insurance companies providing the same type of Benefits, and often resulting in overinsurance.

EARNED INCOME — gross salary, wages, commissions, fees, etc., derived from active employment. This does not include nonearned income, such as income from investments, rents, annuities, insurance policies, etc.

EARNED PREMIUM — that portion of the Premium that applies to the expired portion of the policy term. For example, an insurance company is considered to have earned 75% of an Annual Premium after a period of 9 months of an annual term has elapsed.

ELECTIVE INDEMNITY — fixed lump sum payments which an Insured may elect to receive instead of accepting the Weekly or Monthly Indemnity provided for in the policy. Usually, such payments are made for dislocations, fractures, or for the loss of fingers or toes.

ELIMINATION PERIOD — the period of time after the inception of a disability, during which Benefits are not payable (also referred to as the Waiting Period).

EMERGENCY BENEFITS — refer to Identification Benefits.

ENDORSEMENT — a legal amendment added to the policy by which the scope of coverage is revised, i.e., restricted or increased. The terms of such endorsement (rider) take precedence over the printed portions of the policy which are in conflict with the endorsement.

GLOSSARY OF HEALTH INSURANCE TERMS

EVIDENCE OF INSURABILITY — any statement or proof of a person's physical condition, occupation, etc., affecting the acceptance for insurance.

EXCEPTED PERIOD — refer to Elimination Period.

EXCEPTIONS — provisions in a policy that eliminate coverage for specified losses or causes of loss.

EXCLUSIONS — the same as Exceptions.

EXPERIENCE RATING — the Premium is computed on the basis of past losses and expenses incurred by the insurance company in the settlement of claims and other expenses involving a particular group of risks.

FAMILY EXPENSE POLICY — a policy which insures both the policyholder and his immediate dependents (usually his spouse and children).

FRANCHISE — a method of marketing Health Insurance for certain groups which do not comply with all the criteria of a Group Insurance Plan. Individual Health Policies are issued to the Insureds. The Benefits may vary slightly within the Group.

FRATERNAL INSURANCE — a cooperative type of insurance provided by a social organization for its members.

FREQUENCY — the number of times a specific type of disability occurs.

FREQUENCY RATE — this measures the probability of the occurrence of a disability. Also known as the Incidence Rate (refer to Severity Rate).

GRACE PERIOD — a specified period, after a Premium payment is due, during which the protection of the policy continues even though the payment for the Renewal Premium has not as yet been received.

GROUP CERTIFICATE — refer to Certificate of Insurance.

GROUP INSURANCE POLICY — a policy (generally, called a "Master Policy") protecting a group of persons, usually employees of a firm.

GUARANTEED CONTINUABLE — the same as Guaranteed Renewable.

GUARANTEED RENEWABLE — the option of renewal to a specified age, or for a lifetime, vested solely in the Insured. However, the insurance company has the right to increase the Premiums applicable to an entire class of policyholders.

HEALTH INSURANCE — a broad term covering the various forms of insurance relating to the health of persons. It includes such coverages as Accident, Sickness, Disability, and Hospital and Medical Expense. This term is used instead of Sickness and Accident Insurance.

HEALTH MAINTENANCE ORGANIZATON (HMO) — an organization that provides for a wide range of comprehensive health care services for a specified group in consideration of fixed periodic Premium payments. An HMO may be sponsored by a medical school, hospital, employer, labor union, consumer group, insurance company, hospital-medical plan, or the government.

GLOSSARY OF HEALTH INSURANCE TERMS

HOSPITAL BENEFITS — Benefits payable for charges incurred while the Insured is confined to, or treated in, a hospital, as defined in the policy.

HOSPITAL EXPENSE INSURANCE — Benefits subject to a Specified Daily Maximum for a specified period of time while the Insured is confined to a hospital, plus a limited allowance up to a specified amount for miscellaneous hospital expenses such as operating rooms, anesthesia, laboratory fees, etc.

HOSPITALIZATION INSURANCE — the same as Hospital Expense Insurance.

HOSPITAL MEDICAL INSURANCE — a term used to describe protection which provides Benefits for the cost of any or all of the numerous health care services normally covered under Health Insurance Plans.

IDENTIFICATION BENEFITS — a provision under which the insurance company agrees to pay the expense of putting a disabled Insured in touch with relatives, and placing him in their care. This provision appears rarely in policies issued currently.

IMPAIRED RISK — refer to Risk.

INCONTESTABLE CLAUSE — (Time Limit on Certain Defenses) a clause which makes the policy indisputable regarding the statements made by the Insured in the application after a specified period of time has elapsed (usually two or three years).

INDEMNITY — the payment of a Benefit for a loss insured under a policy. The Insured is indemnified for a specified loss, or part thereof.

INDIVIDUAL INSURANCE — policies which afford protection to the policyholder and/or his family (as distinct from Group Insurance or Blanket Insurance). Sometimes it is called Personal Insurance.

INDUSTRIAL POLICY — a policy providing nominal indemnities for a short period of time, and the Premiums for which are usually payable weekly or monthly.

INJURY INDEPENDENT OF ALL OTHER MEANS — an injury resulting from an accident, provided that the accident was not caused by an illness.

INPATIENT — a person who is admitted to a hospital as a resident case (i.e., as a bed patient).

INSURABLE INTEREST — relationship between the Insured and the Beneficiary, i.e., one of blood, marriage, or economic dependence.

INSURANCE — protection in accordance with a written contract against the financial hazards (in whole or in part) of the happening of specified fortuitous events.

INSURANCE COMPANY, ALIEN — one that was organized under the laws of a country other than the United States.

GLOSSARY OF HEALTH INSURANCE TERMS

INSURANCE COMPANY, DOMESTIC — one conducting business in the State in which it was organized.

INSURANCE COMPANY, FOREIGN — one conducting business in a State other than the State in which it was organized.

INSURED — the person on whom an insurance policy is written.

INSURED PERCENTAGE — refer to Coinsurance.

INSURING CLAUSE — a clause which defines and describes the scope of the coverage afforded and the limits of indemnification.

INTEGRATED DEDUCTIBLE — a Deductible which is determined as a fixed amount or the sum of the Benefits paid under all other coverages for the same loss, whichever is greater.

INTERNAL LIMITS — a restriction on the amount of the Benefit for a specific type of care (or treatment) irrespective of the maximum amount of Benefits (or Coinsured Benefits) that would be paid for all types of eligible expenses.

KEY MAN INSURANCE — an Individual Policy (or Group Insurance) designed to protect an essential employee(s) of a firm against the loss of income resulting from disability. If desired, it may be written for the benefit of the employer, who usually continues to pay the salary during periods of disability.

LAPSE — termination of a policy upon the policyholder's failure to pay the Premium within the time required.

LEVEL PREMIUM — a Premium which remains unchanged throughout the life of a policy.

LIFETIME DISABILITY BENEFIT — a payment to help replace income lost by an Insured for as long as he is totally disabled.

LIMITED POLICIES — those which restrict Benefits to specified accidents or diseases, such as Travel Accident Policies, Ticket Insurance Policies, etc.

LONG-TERM DISABILITY INCOME INSURANCE — a provision to pay Benefits to a covered disabled person as long as he remains disabled up to a specific policy Benefit period; generally, exceeding two to five years.

LOSS-OF-INCOME (TIME) BENEFITS — Income Benefits payable to the Insured because he is unable to work due to an insured disability.

LOSS-OF-INCOME INSURANCE — policies which provide Benefits to help replace an Insured's earned income lost or curtailed as a result of an illness or an accident.

LOSS OF SIGHT — the entire and irrecoverable loss of sight of one or both eyes.

GLOSSARY OF HEALTH INSURANCE TERMS

Loss Reserves — refer to Claim Reserves.

Major Medical Expense Insurance — policies specially designed to help offset the heavy medical expenses resulting from catastrophic or prolonged illnesses or injuries. Generally, they provide Benefit payments of 75-80% of all types of medical expenses above a certain amount first paid by the Insured, and up to the Maximum Limit of Liability provided by the policy, e.g., $100,000.

Malingering — prolonging a disability in order to collect greater Insurance Benefits.

Master Policy — represents the entire policy in Group Insurance and spells out the agreement between the employer (or a union, association, or a trustee) and the insurance company.

Medicaid — a State Medical Assistance Program for eligible needy persons.

Medical Attendance — treatment or care by a legally qualified physician.

Medical Expense Insurance — policies which provide Benefits for doctors' fees for nonsurgical care commonly rendered in a hospital, and visits at home or at physicians' offices. Sometimes, these Benefits are afforded under Hospital and Surgical Expense Policies.

Medicare — a program of Health Insurance and medical care for persons who are 65 years of age or over, and certain other disabled persons under age 65 operated under the provisions of the Social Security Act.

Minimum Indemnities For Specified Losses — fixed minimum lump sum payments for specified losses. Usually, such payments are made for loss of fingers or toes, and for fractures and dislocations.

Miscellaneous Expenses — hospital charges other than room-and-board; i.e., X-rays, drugs, laboratory fees, etc. (in connection with Hospital Insurance).

Misrepresentation — a false statement which the prospective Insured makes in an application for a policy. A misrepresentation is material if the insurance company, having known the true facts, would have refused to issue the policy. Statements are considered representations and not warranties.

Moral Hazards — habits, morals, or financial practices of an Insured which increase the possibility or extent of a loss.

Morbidity Table — shows the incidence and extent of disability which may be expected from a given large group of persons. This table is used in the computation of rates. It is comparable to a Mortality Table used in connection with Life Insurance.

GLOSSARY OF HEALTH INSURANCE TERMS

MUTUAL HEALTH INSURANCE COMPANY — a Health Insurance Company owned and controlled by its policyholders. Mutual Health Insurance Companies issue Participating Policies.

NEWSPAPER POLICIES — a type of limited Accident Policy. Usually, it is purchased through a newspaper concurrently with a subscription, and the Premiums are collected by the newspaper delivery man.

NONCANCELLABLE POLICY — a policy which an insurance company is not permitted to terminate or amend during its term (except for nonpayment of a Premium). Usually, the renewal of the policy is guaranteed at the option of the Insured to a specified age at a fixed Premium.

NONCANCELLABLE AND GUARANTEED RENEWABLE POLICY — refer to "Noncancellable Policy".

NONCONFINING SICKNESS — that which prevents the Insured from working, but does not confine him to his home, a hospital, or a sanitarium.

NONCONTRIBUTORY GROUP PLANS — plans under which the employer pays the entire Premium.

NONDISABLING INJURY — one which requires medical care but does not result in a loss of time from work.

NONOCCUPATIONAL POLICY — a policy which insures a person against off-the-job accidents or sicknesses.

NONPARTICIPATING INSURANCE — insurance which does not pay dividends to the policyholders.

NONPROFIT INSURERS — entities organized under special State Laws to provide Hospital, Medical, or Dental Insurance on a nonprofit basis.

NONPRORATING — the Benefits in the policy will not be changed, or the amount of coverage reduced, because of any change in occupation to one which is more hazardous, the existence of other insurance covering the same loss, or the falsification of age in the application for insurance. The policies of some insurance companies contain a Nonprorating Clause which applies only to a change of occupation.

OCCUPATIONAL CLASSIFICATION — a list of occupations classified according to the degree of hazard incident to each particular type of work. The classifications are based upon a statistical analysis of the frequency and severity of claims. Occupations are separated into several groups, each group having the same relative degree of hazard.

OCCUPATIONAL HAZARD — a hazard inherent in the Insured's type of work.

OLDER AGE OR SENIOR CITIZEN POLICY — one which is issued to an applicant who is over 65 years of age. These policies supplement the coverage afforded by the government under the Medicare Program.

GLOSSARY OF HEALTH INSURANCE TERMS

OPTIONAL BENEFIT — an additional Benefit which may be included in a policy at the applicant's request.

OPTIONAL INDEMNITY — refer to Elective Indemnity.

OPTIONAL RENEWABLE POLICIES — policies which are renewable at the option of the insurance company.

OUTLINE OF BENEFITS — refer to Disclosure Statement.

OUTPATIENT — one who receives care at a clinic or hospital without being confined to that institution as a resident patient.

OVERHEAD EXPENSE INSURANCE (BUSINESS OR PROFESSIONAL OVERHEAD EXPENSE INSURANCE) — a form of insurance which reimburses a sole proprietor (or a professional man) for the overhead expenses that must be paid even when he is disabled.

OVERINSURANCE — an excessive amount of insurance carried by an Insured which might tempt him to prolong his period of disability, remain in a hospital longer than necessary, etc.

PARTIAL DISABILITY — generally defined as an illness or injury which prevents an Insured from performing one or more of his occupational duties.

PARTICIPATING INSURANCE — insurance which entitles the policyholder to share in the divisible surplus of the insurance company through dividends.

PERCENTAGE PARTICIPATION — refer to Coinsurance.

PERMANENT DISABILITY — a disability that is expected to continue for the lifetime of the disabled person.

PERSONAL INSURANCE — the same as Individual Insurance.

PHYSICAL HAZARD — that type of hazard which arises from the physical characteristics of an individual. It may exist because of past medical history, physical condition present at birth, or a current condition.

POLICY FEE — the small sum charged by some insurance companies for the first year (or portion thereof) in addition to the regular Premium.

POLICY RESERVE — an additional reserve for a Noncancellable Policy required by law (also known as the Level Premium Reserve).

POLICY TERM — the period of time for which the policy will normally remain in existence.

PRE-EXISTING CONDITION — an injury, sickness, or physical condition which existed prior to the issuance of a Health Policy.

PREMIUM — the periodic payment required to keep a policy in force.

GLOSSARY OF HEALTH INSURANCE TERMS

PREPAID GROUP PRACTICE PLAN — a plan under which specified health services are rendered by participating physicians to an enrolled group of persons, with fixed periodic Premium payments made in advance by or on behalf of each covered person or family. If a Health Insurance company is involved, it contracts to pay in advance for the full range of health services to which the Insured is entitled under the terms of the Health Insurance Contract.

PRINCIPAL SUM — the amount payable for loss of life.

PRIOR ORIGINS — refers to a disability, the cause of which occurred before the effective date of the policy.

PROBATIONARY PERIOD — a specified number of days after the date of the issuance of the policy, during which coverage is not afforded for sickness. Sickness Protection does not become effective until after the end of such Probationary Period. Sickness contracted during the Probationary Period is not covered regardless of the duration of such disability.

PRO RATA UNEARNED PREMIUM — if the insurance company cancels a policy, the amount of the Returned Premium is proportional to the unexpired period for which the Premium had been paid in advance.

PRO RATA UNEARNED PREMIUM RESERVE — a reserve required by Law because Premiums are paid in advance and are only earned by the insurance company over the policy period for which protection has been afforded (the unearned portion of the Premium representing a liability to the policyholders).

PRORATION — the reduction in the amount of Benefits payable because the Insured has changed to a more hazardous occupation since the issuance of the policy, because of the existence of additional insurance covering the same loss, or because of a misstatement of age.

QUALIFIED IMPAIRMENT INSURANCE — a form of substandard or special class of insurance that restricts the Benefits because of the Insured's particular stipulated undesirable condition of health.

QUARANTINE INDEMNITY — a Monthly Benefit payable while the Insured is involuntarily quarantined because of exposure to a contagious disease.

REBATING — paying, offering to pay or allow, the giving of anything of value, or any valuable consideration not specified in the policy to any person as an inducement to apply for and secure a policy of insurance. Rebating is illegal.

RECURRENT DISABILITY CLAUSE — a provision which specifies a period of time during which the recurrence of a condition is considered a continuation of a prior period of disability or hospital confinement.

REDUCTION OF BENEFITS — automatic reduction in coverage under certain specified conditions, e.g., the Monthly Benefits may be reduced by 50% while a female Insured ceases to be fully and gainfully employed away from home, or after the Insured has reached age 60 or 65.

GLOSSARY OF HEALTH INSURANCE TERMS

REIMBURSEMENT — the amount the insurance company will pay for the actual expenses incurred by the Insured subject to a stipulated maximum.

REINSTATEMENT — the resumption of coverage under a policy which had been lapsed.

RELATION OF EARNINGS TO INSURANCE — refer to Average Earnings Clause.

RENEWAL — continuance of coverage under a policy beyond its original term.

REPRESENTATIONS — an oral or written statement made by an applicant to an insurance company for the issuance of an insurance policy. A representation need be only substantially true when made. State laws require that all statements made by the applicant in his application for insurance be construed as representations.

RESERVE — a sum (required by law) set aside by an insurance company to assure the payment of future claims.

RESIDUAL DISABILITY BENEFIT — a provision which states that if an Insured returns to his regular occupation and his income is reduced because he is disabled, the insurance company will pay a reduced Benefit for as long as the Insured's income is reduced because of his disability. There are a number of variations of this Benefit.

RETROACTIVE WAIVER OF PREMIUM — a provision under which the payment of Premiums are waived after a disability has continued for a specified period (e.g., 60 days, 90 days, or 6 months). Any Premiums paid during that period are refunded to the Insured.

RIDER — refer to Endorsement.

RISK (IMPAIRED OR SUBSTANDARD) — an applicant whose physical condition does not meet the normal minimum standards for normal health.

SCHEDULE — a list of specific maximum amounts payable, usually for surgical operations, dismemberments, etc.

SCHEDULE TYPE POLICY — includes a listing and a complete text of the provisions of each of several Benefits, most of which are optional, and some of which may be omitted at the election of the applicant.

SENIOR CITIZEN OR OLDER AGE POLICY — one which is issued to an applicant who is over 65 years of age. These policies supplement the coverage afforded by the government under the Medicare Program.

SERVICE BENEFITS — those Benefits which are received in the form of specified hospital or medical care rather than in terms of cash amounts.

SEVERITY RATE — the average severity of a disability (refer to Frequency Rate).

GLOSSARY OF HEALTH INSURANCE TERMS

SHORT RATE TABLE — if an Insured cancels his policy, the Earned Premium is calculated by the use of a Short Rate Table. It provides for the return of less than the Pro Rata Unearned Premium to the Insured, reimbursing the insurance company (in part) for the expense incurred in connection with the issuance of the policy.

SHORT-TERM DISABILITY INCOME INSURANCE — a provision to pay Benefits to a covered disabled person as long as he remains disabled up to a specified (short) period; generally, not exceeding two to five years.

SPECIAL CLASS — an applicant who cannot qualify for a standard policy, but may secure one with an endorsement (rider) waiving the payment for a loss involving certain existing health impairments. He may be required to pay a higher Premium, or to accept a policy of a type other than the one for which he had applied.

SPECIAL RISK INSURANCE — supplies coverage for risks or hazards of an unusual nature.

STANDARD PROVISIONS — certain provisions which must be included in any Health Policy. Originally, there were 15 Mandatory Provisions and 8 Optional Provisions. In 1950, these were replaced by new Uniform Provisions of which there are 12 Mandatory Provisions and 11 Optional Provisions. The 1950 provisions have been adopted by most States.

STATUTORY DISABILITY BENEFITS LAW — the States of California, Hawaii, New Jersey, New York, Rhode Island, and the Commonwealth of Puerto Rico have laws which compel employers (under specified conditions) to provide insurance for their employees to afford coverage for the loss of income (and in some cases medical expenses) resulting from nonoccupational accidents or sickness. The insurance may be obtained from a private insurance company, a State Fund, or may be afforded under an approved Self-Insurance Plan.

STOCK INSURANCE COMPANY — an insurance company owned and controlled by its stockholders.

SUBSTANDARD RISK — refer to Risk.

SURGICAL EXPENSE INSURANCE — a policy which provides Benefits to pay for the cost of operations.

SURGICAL SCHEDULE — a list of maximum cash allowances which are payable for various types of surgery based upon the severity of the operations performed.

TICKET INSURANCE — protection which is issued in conjunction with a ticket for transportation on a common carrier.

TIME LIMIT ON CERTAIN DEFENSES — a required Uniform Provision which prohibits an insurance company from contesting the validity of the policy, or from denying a claim for disability commencing (or loss incurred) after 2 years (sometimes 3 years) from the date of issuance on the ground that the applicant had made misstatements (except fraudulent misstatements) in the application. In Guaranteed Renewable and

GLOSSARY OF HEALTH INSURANCE TERMS

Noncancellable Policies, the insurance company may omit the parenthetical phrase "(except fraudulent misstatements)". This is somewhat similar to the Incontestable Clause in a Life Insurance Policy.

TIME LIMIT — the period of time in which a Notice of Claim or Proof of Loss must be filed.

TOTAL DISABILITY — an illness or injury which prevents an Insured from continuously performing every duty pertaining to his occupation or from engaging in any other type of work for remuneration. (This wording varies from one insurance company to another.)

TRAVEL-ACCIDENT INSURANCE — provides Benefits for accidental injury while traveling, usually on a common carrier.

TWISTING — inducing an Insured to cancel his present insurance and replace it with insurance in the same or another insurance company by misrepresenting the facts or by presenting an incomplete comparison.

UNALLOCATED BENEFIT — reimbursement up to a maximum amount for the cost of extra hospital services, but not specifying the exact amount to be paid for each charge. (This is often referred to as a Blanket Benefit.)

UNAUTHORIZED COMPANY — one which is not licensed in a State in which it operates.

WAITING PERIOD — refer to Elimination Period.

WAIVER — an agreement which waives the liability of the insurance company for a loss which would normally be covered under the policy.

WAIVER OF PREMIUM — a provision included in many policies which waives the payment of Premiums after an Insured has been totally disabled for a specified period, e.g., 90 days (180 days in some policies).

WARRANTY — a warranty must be literally true. A breach of warranty may be sufficient to void the policy whether the warranty is material or not and whether or not such warranty had contributed to the loss.

WORKERS' COMPENSATION — Benefits paid for an injury (or disease contracted) arising out of and in the course of employment. The amount of the Benefits and the conditions under which employees are eligible are determined by the Workers' Compensation Law. In most States, insurance providing these Benefits may be purchased from private insurance companies. In a few States, only a Monopolistic State Workers' Compensation Fund is permitted to issue such insurance. In some States, the coverage may be obtained from either a State Fund or from a private insurance company.

WRITTEN PREMIUMS — the total amount of Premiums on all policies issued by an insurance company.

SELF-QUIZ

The following questions (multiple choice) are comparable to those appearing on State examinations for prospective Health Insurance Agents. However, if your copy of the Health Insurance Primer contains a special Addendum applicable to your State, the Review Questions contained in that Addendum should be studied before taking the following Self-Quiz.

If there appears to be more than one acceptable answer, select the one which is most suitable for the situation involved.

1. *Which one of the following statements pertaining to Medicare is incorrect? Plan B is a Supplementary Plan that:*

........a. Is subject to a calendar year Deductible before any payments are rendered

........b. Pays 80% of incurred necessary and reasonable costs of out-patient health services such as: X-rays, laboratory services, surgical dressings, and appliances

........c. Is a mandatory coverage provided to all Medicare recipients enrolled in Plan A

........d. Is voluntary and is financed from monthly Premiums paid by enrollees and by the general revenues of the Federal Government

2. *If an Agent knew that a prospect was a moral hazard, which of the following should he do?*

........a. Complete the application

........b. Complete the application with a Waiver Rider

........c. Ask the applicant to promise to correct the condition and then complete the application

........d. Refuse to complete the application

3. *Which of the following actions would be taken by an insurance company with respect to the issuance of a policy for an applicant who is considered a moral hazard? It would:*

........a. Issue a policy if the applicant promised to correct the hazard

........b. Not issue a policy

........c. Issue a Substandard Policy

........d. Issue a policy with a Waiver Rider

4. *Mr. Jones has a full-time 40-hour-week position as an office worker and a part-time position of 20 hours a week as a construction worker. Which classification would be applied?*

       I The full-time position
      II The part-time position
     III The least hazardous position
     IV The most hazardous position

SELF-QUIZ

........a. IV ....c. III
........b. II and IV ....d. I and III

5. *Under the Double Indemnity Provision, all of the following Benefits would be doubled except:*

........a. Dismemberment ....c. Medical Expenses
........b. Accidental Death ....d. Weekly Income Payments

6. *Under the Elective Indemnities Provision, all of the following would apply except:*

........a. Dislocated shoulder ....c. Loss of a toe
........b. Fractured arm ....d. Punctured lung

7. *The Principal Sum would be paid for which one of the following:*

........a. Dismemberment of both feet
........b. Total Disability
........c. Irrevocable loss of sight of both eyes
........d. Accidental Death

8. *All of the following would be eligible to be Beneficiaries except:*

........a. Children by a former marriage
........b. Brothers and sisters
........c. Someone who owes you money
........d. Someone to whom you owe money

9. *If a policy did not contain the name of a Beneficiary, the payment would be made to:*

........a. The wife
........b. The children
........c. The Insured's brothers and sisters
........d. The Insured's estate

10. *If the Insured desires to change an Irrevocable Beneficiary what action would you take?*

........a. Have the Insured sign a Change of Beneficiary Form
........b. Have a doctor sign a Change of Beneficiary Form
........c. Have the Secondary Beneficiary sign a Change of Beneficiary Form
........d. Have the Beneficiary and Insured sign a Change of Beneficiary Form

SELF-QUIZ

11. *If a policy has a 14-day Probationary Period with a 7-day Elimination Period, under which of the following circumstances would the Insured be able to collect?*

........a. The Insured became ill 13 days after the effective date of the policy and was ill for two weeks

........b. The Insured became ill 7 days after the effective date of the policy and was ill for 21 days

........c. The Insured was ill for 7 days after the 45th day after the effective date of the policy

........d. The Insured was ill for 25 days after the 14th day after the effective date of the policy

12. *If an Insured has $500 Blanket Medical Expense Coverage and his hospital and medical expenses were $460, how much would the insurance company pay?*

........a. $460 ....c. $500
........b. $410 ....d. $450

13. *If an insurance company wants to cancel a policy how much notice must be given to the Insured?*

........a. 10 days ....c. 60 days
........b. 30 days ....d. 90 days

14. *Must members of a Group prove insurability?*

........a. No

........b. Yes, if the majority of the Group are women

........c. Yes, if they are in a hazardous occupation

........d. Yes, if they are over age 50

15. *Members of a Group are notified that they are insured by the:*

........a. Issuance of a policy

........b. Issuance of a certificate

........c. Employer

........d. Insurance company by mail

16. *Are officers of a corporation eligible for membership in a Group?*

........a. No, they must be insured individually

........b. Yes, if the Plan is contributory

........c. Yes, if they are salaried members of the corporation

SELF-QUIZ

........d. Yes, if they are in a nonhazardous occupation

17. *Who can change the phraseology in a policy?*

........a. The Agent
........b. The Insured
........c. An executive officer of an insurance company
........d. No one

18. *For whom is Overhead Insurance designed?*

........a. Small proprietorships ....c. Salesmen
........b. Truck drivers ....d. Large corporations

19. *A Noncancellable and Guaranteed Renewable Policy:*

........a. Is the same as a Guaranteed Renewable Policy
........b. Can be renewed only when the guarantee period is in effect
........c. Must be renewed (up to age stated in the policy) as long as the Insured pays his Premiums, and the insurance company does not have the right to increase the Premiums
........d. Must be renewed for the lifetime of the Insured, but the Premium may be increased at specified intervals

20. *Is a Grace Period required in all Health Policies?*

........a. Yes ....c. Optional
........b. No ....d. Only in Income Policies

21. *What are the moral obligations of an Agent to an Insured?*

    I To aid him with the settlement of claims
    II To help him select the right coverage for his needs
    III To keep him informed of all the latest developments in his insurance coverage and to keep his coverage up-to-date
    IV To make certain that coverage for dependents is added when necessary

........a. I, II, and III ....c. I, III, and IV
........b. I ....d. All of the above

22. *Which of the following statements pertaining to Medicare is least correct?*

........a. Basic Plan A is financed by a payroll tax on the employees and employers who are required to make regular Social Security contributions.

SELF-QUIZ

.......b. Basic Plan A pays for all hospital services normally furnished to inpatients including the cost of room and board in semi-private accommodations, less a specified Deductible.

.......c. In addition to the above, Plan A also pays for the services (if received in a hospital) of physicians, surgeons, and private nurses.

.......d. Basic Plan A of Medicare is administered by fiscal intermediaries and Supplementary Plan B is administered by carriers. Fiscal intermediaries are selected by the providers and approved by the Social Security Administration. The carriers are selected by the Social Security Administration on a geographic basis.

23. *An Insured has a Major Medical Policy with a $250 Deductible, a 75%-25% Coinsurance Clause with an aggregate total of $7,500. He incurs covered medical bills amounting to $4,500. How much would the insurance company pay?*

.......a. $4,500 ....c. $3,187.50
.......b. $1,062.50 ....d. $4,250

24. *Key Man Insurance may be issued to afford coverage for:*

   I Important employees of the business
   II The loss of business due to the disabilities of key personnel
   III Disability of the owner of the business
   IV Disability of a partner in a business

   The most correct answer is:

.......a. III ....c. I, III, and IV
.......b. I, II, and III ....d. All of the above

25. *Which job classification is considered the least hazardous?*

.......a. Office clerk ....c. Railroad worker
.......b. Construction worker ....d. Real estate agent

26. *Earned Income is income derived from:*

.......a. Salaries, commissions, and bonuses
.......b. Dividends and interest
.......c. Salary, interest, and dividends
.......d. Stocks, bonds, and real estate

27. *Which of the following Benefits are derived from the ownership of a Health Policy?*

   I Conserves savings

SELF-QUIZ

    II Alleviates the necessity of borrowing money
    III Gives the Insured peace of mind and relieves him of emotional strain
    IV Helps pay medical expenses
    V Accumulates cash value

........a. I, II, and V
........b. I, III, and IV
........c. All of the above except V
........d. All of the above except III and V

28. *A man would be considered Totally Disabled if he couldn't:*

........a. Perform any and all of his usual duties
........b. Perform any and all of his important duties
........c. Perform one or more of his important daily duties
........d. Attend to his business for 50% or more of his usual time

29. *An Agent may share his commissions with:*

........a. His client
........b. Any licensed Agent of any other licensed insurance company
........c. Another licensed Agent of the same insurance company
........d. No one

30. *When an Agent returns his commissions to a client this is called:*

........a. Waiver of Premium   ....c. Rebating
........b. Twisting   ....d. Issuance of a Waiver

31. *The following information would be important in connection with the underwriting of a policy:*

    I Age
    II Income
    III Occupation
    IV Hobbies
    V Previous medical history

........a. I and II
........b. All of the above except IV
........c. All of the above except II
........d. All of the above

32. *An insurance company's advertisement must disclose the following information:*

SELF-QUIZ

........a. Total assets
........b. Dividends paid annually
........c. Full name of the insurance company and the location of the home office
........d. Liabilities

33. *When explaining dividends the following information must be supplied:*

........a. That they are not guaranteed
........b. The dividends paid in previous years
........c. The anticipated dividends
........d. The relation to the cost of the policy

34. *The Coinsurance Provision in a Hospital or Major Medical Policy has the following purpose:*

........a. To give the Insured full coverage
........b. To eliminate unnecessary use of medical services by the Insured by having him pay 20% or 25% of the bills
........c. To make sure that the hospital or doctor receives full payment
........d. All of the above

35. *Double Indemnity will be paid if the Insured sustains bodily injury:*

........a. By the explosion of a steamboiler
........b. By a hurricane or a tornado
........c. While a passenger in or on a public conveyance provided by a common carrier for passenger service
........d. All of the above

36. *A Contributory Group Health Policy must cover:*

    I 100% of all eligible employees
    II All employees within a class of employees
    III At least 75% of the eligible employees
    IV Any eligible employee who wishes to participate

The most correct answer is:

......a. I   ....c. III and IV
......b. II   ....d. IV

37. *A Blanket Health Policy is:*

........a. A contract of insurance issued against death or injury from

SELF-QUIZ

sickness and/or accident insuring a group of persons exposed to a common hazard

........b. An insurance contract covering all hospital and medical expenses up to a maximum established in the policy

........c. The same as Blanket Medical Expense

........d. The same as Common Carrier Insurance

38. *Which of the following is the reason one clerk would be rated AAA and the other rated B even though they are the same age?*

........a. One is nearsighted and must wear glasses — the other has 20-20 vision

........b. One is 6'2" and the other is 5'4"

........c. One is a bank clerk and the other is a clerk working at a construction site

........d. One has a good family health history and the other has a poor family health history

39. *Can the rates of a Guaranteed Renewable Policy be changed?*

........a. Yes, at predetermined intervals

........b. No, not as long as the Insured pays the Premium when due

........c. Yes, on a class basis only

........d. Yes, if the insurance company paid too many claims under the policy

40. *Which of the following statements are correct? The Grace Period is:*

      I The period of time following the date that the Premium is due, during which coverage is continued

      II The period of time following the inception of the policy during which the Premium may be paid late

      III The time between receipt of the Premium Notice and the time that payment is made

      IV 7 days on a Weekly Premium Policy; 10 days on a Monthly Premium Policy; 31 days on all others

........a. I ....c. IV

........b. II and IV ....d. I and IV

41. *A Notice of Claim must be given to the insurance company within 20 days except:*

........a. Sundays and holidays

........b. If the injuries are caused by an automobile accident

SELF-QUIZ

.........c. If the Insured is unable to do so; however, he must file the claim as soon thereafter as is reasonably possible

.........d. No exceptions, it must be done within 20 days

42. *Which of the following statements pertaining to adverse selection are correct? Adverse selection:*

    I Is selection against the insurance company

    II Is the underwriting duty of the insurance company

    III Is in favor of the insurance company

    IV Is the tendency of poor risks to buy more insurance

    V Has to do with the insurance company's selection of applicants

.........a. III and V   ....c. I and IV

.........b. IV   ....d. II and V

43. *After determining that an Insured's Benefit payments exceeded his Average Monthy Income and he came under the Average Earnings Clause in his policy, the insurance company may:*

.........a. Reduce the Benefits payable but not to a figure which is less than $200 a month with no return of Premium

.........b. Reduce the Benefit payments to his Average Earnings Level (but not less than $200 a month) and return the difference in Premium (Unearned Premium)

.........c. Not pay Benefits lower than his Average Earnings plus one-half of his Benefits

.........d. Take the Insured before an Insurance Commission panel for a settlement which is binding on both

44. *A misrepresentation is not material unless it led the insurance company to issue coverage that would not have been issued if the true facts had been known. This statement is:*

.........a. False

.........b. Valid only if there was a witness

.........c. True

.........d. False, a misrepresentation is always material

45. *An Insuring Agreement:*

.........a. Defines the Limits of Liability

.........b. Specifies how much the Insured will receive

.........c. Defines the conditions under which Benefits will be paid (subject to the exclusions and limitations)

SELF-QUIZ

.........d. Binds the insurance company to the risk

46. *A Probationary Period is:*

.........a. The same as a Waiting Period
.........b. The same as an Elimination Period
.........c. 14 days
.........d. The period of time between the effective date of the policy and the date Sickness Coverage becomes effective

47. *A Commercial Policy is:*

.........a. Written on an individual engaged in a hazardous occupation
.........b. Sold to commercial industry only
.........c. Written to cover a person in a nonhazardous occupation with high limits and long periods of coverage
.........d. Covers people engaged in interstate commerce

48. *In a Noncancellable and Guaranteed Renewable Policy, the insurance company:*

.........a. May change Benefits on a class basis but may not refuse to renew
.........b. May not cancel or refuse to renew as long as the Insured pays the Premium and the insurance company does not have the right to increase the Premiums
.........c. May refuse to renew the policy for stipulated reasons
.........d. May change the policy from time to time but **must** renew

49. *A Health Insurance Policy is:*

.........a. Issued every year
.........b. Issued every three years
.........c. A policy which covers only loss of income due to sickness
.........d. A contract between an insurance company and an Insured under which the insurance company agrees to pay certain Benefits to the Insured or his Beneficiary for specified losses sustained by the Insured, resulting from sickness or injury

50. *An unforeseen, unexpected, and unintended cause of an accident which results in an injury is the definition of:*

.........a. Accidental bodily injury ....c. Accidental means
.........b. Unexpected means ....d. Accidental result

51. *The methods of payment under a Health Policy are:*

.........a. Income payments paid weekly or monthly

132

SELF-QUIZ

........b. Lump sum payments paid as specified

........c. Reimbursements for specified expenses

........d. All of the above

52. *Which of the following statements pertaining to a Waiver of Premium Provision are correct?*

  I It relieves the Insured of the obligation of paying Premiums

  II It is a mandatory provision in Health Policies

  III The Insured must be Totally Disabled (within the requirements of the policy) in order to be eligible for this provision

  IV If the Insured recovers from his Total Disability, he must reimburse the insurance company for the Premiums that were waived

........a. I   ....c. I and III

........b. III and IV   ....d. I, III, and IV

53. *The Elective Indemnities Benefit is applicable if the Insured suffers a dislocation, fracture, or amputation of fingers or toes. This is advantageous because:*

........a. The bodily injury may not disable the Insured

........b. A lump sum paid might be greater than the Income Benefit

........c. The Insured may elect to receive the lump sum payment in lieu of the Income Benefit

........d. All of the above

54. *After an applicant has paid the initial Premium and accepted delivery of a Health Policy, he:*

........a. May return it within ten days and receive a full refund of the Premium paid

........b. Must get written permission to return the policy for a refund

........c. May obtain a refund less the medical fee, if any, if he returns the policy within ten days

........d. Must keep it at least for the term it was issued

55. *An Agent has an Insurance Special Premium (Bank) Account. Which of the following is he permitted to do with this account?*

  I Pay his office operation bills from it

  II Deposit other funds in it to maintain an adequate balance

  III Forward Return Premiums to his clients

  IV Forward payment of Premiums to the insurance company

  V Use it as his business account to save extra charges

SELF-QUIZ

The most correct answer is:

........a. I, III, and V ....c. I, II, III, and IV
........b. II, III, and IV ....d. II

56. *After reinstatement of a Health Policy, the Insured is covered for:*

   I Sickness and accident immediately
   II Sickness after ten days
   III Accident after ten days
   IV Accident immediately

The most correct answer is:

........a. I and III ....c. I
........b. II and IV ....d. II and III

57. *A policy is issued with a Waiver (Impairment) Endorsement. Would you advise the prospective Insured to:*

........a. Accept it because it merely excludes a pre-existing condition and he is covered for everything else
........b. Accept it because you promise that you will have the insurance company remove it at a later date
........c. Refuse it and try another insurance company
........d. Write a letter to the insurance company demanding its removal

58. *An applicant validates the answers on his application by:*

........a. Checking all questions
........b. Signing where indicated and initialing all corrections
........c. Taking a medical examination
........d. Accepting the policy when issued and signing all Waivers

59. *An Insured has a Health Policy with a surgical schedule that affords a maximum Benefit payment of $250 on any number of operations resulting from one injury. He will be reimbursed for the actual costs up to the amount set forth in the surgical schedule. The Insured has two dissimilar operations (due to the same injury) at different times. The first one cost $100 and the second cost $125. The schedule indicates that the maximum payment for the first type of operation is $100 and for the second type of operation it is $150. The Insured would receive a total of:*

........a. $250
........b. $100 for the first and $25 for the second
........c. $225
........d. $100 less $50 for the first and $125 less $50 for the second

SELF-QUIZ

60. *An Insured stated his age on his application as 30 years. Five years later, he had a claim and it was discovered that he was actually 25 years of age at the time he completed the application. The insurance company would:*

........a. Pay his claim and refund the Excess Premium

........b. Pay his claim according to the amount that the Premium would have purchased based upon his correct age

........c. Not pay the claim and refund all Premiums

........d. Pay the claim but in accordance with the Incontestible Clause, would make no refund

61. *An insurance company may limit its liability by including the following provisions except:*

........a. Change of Occupation

........b. Insurance with Other Insurers

........c. Relation of Earnings to Insurance

........d. Conformity with State Statutes

62. *An employer may use the following factors in determining a class of employees for Group Insurance:*

    I Conditions of employment
    II Location of employment
    III Nature or length of employment
    IV Sex of employees
    V Hourly or weekly remuneration

The most correct answer is:

........a. II and III   ....c. I, II, III, and V

........b. II, IV, and V   ....d. All of the above

63. *Which of the following statements pertaining to a Substandard Health Policy are correct?*

    I It is issued to an applicant who has a substandard income
    II It is issued to an applicant who is a greater risk because of a physical and/or medical condition
    III Usually, it is issued for lower Benefits and the duration of payments may be shorter
    IV It may contain a Waiver (Impairment) Endorsement

........a. I and II   ....c. II and III

........b. II, III, and IV   ....d. All of the above

SELF-QUIZ

64. *Which of the following statements is correct? A Group Health Policy is:*

........a. A policy covering two or more persons

........b. A policy written to cover one or more persons

........c. The same as a Commercial Policy

........d. A policy that covers a number of individuals exposed to the same hazards

65. *A person who acts in any way for an insurance company not licensed in his State is:*

........a. Violating the Insurance Law

........b. Violating the Penal Law

........c. Both of the above

........d. Guilty of a felony

66. *The Medicare Program:*

    I Is a form of Health Insurance available to most persons who are age 65 or over and to certain disabled persons under age 65

    II Is a program of Health care for eligible indigent persons (or families) whether they are working or not

    III Consists of two parts, i.e., Basic Plan A and Supplementary Plan B

    IV Is a form of Health Insurance limited to retirees over age 65 who are receiving Monthly Social Security Payments

The most nearly correct answer is:

........a. I and III   ....c. III and IV

........b. II and III   ....d. None of the above

67. *An Insured has a Health Policy which affords Benefits of $30 weekly and stipulates that the Insured must notify the insurance company if he obtains Health Insurance with other insurance companies. The Insured took out another policy with a second insurance company that afforded $60 Weekly Benefits and did not notify the first insurance company. If he suffered a disability, how much would the first insurance company be required to pay?*

........a. $30 weekly   ....c. $10 weekly

........b. $15 weekly   ....d. $20 weekly

68. *A Waiver (Impairment) Endorsement is attached to a Health Policy to exclude a pre-existing condition for which of the following reasons?*

SELF-QUIZ

    I To enable the insurance company to cover the Insured for other disabilities
    II To permit the insurance company to charge more money
    III To enable the insurance company to issue a policy that it otherwise would not be willing to issue
    IV In order to be fair to both the Insured and the insurance company

The most correct answer is:

........a. I, II, and III   ....c. I, III, and IV
........b. II, III, and IV   ....d. I and III

69. *An insurable interest exists in the following instances:*

    I In the love and affection of persons related by blood or by law
    II If a person is interested in the well being of another person
    III If a person is interested in buying insurance on another person
    IV If a person has an economic interest in the Insured even though he is not related to the Insured

The most correct answer is:

........a. All of the above   ....c. I and IV
........b. I, II, and III   ....d. I, III, and IV

70. *The Capital Sum is the lump sum paid in the event of:*

........a. Accidental death
........b. The loss of all the fingers of one hand and all the toes of one foot
........c. Accidental dismemberment
........d. Compound fracture of an arm or a leg

71. *A Comprehensive Major Medical Policy is:*

........a. Designed to give the protection afforded under both a Basic Hospital Policy and a Major Medical Policy
........b. One that affords coverage for all dental expenses
........c. A policy that provides both Income and Hospital Benefits
........d. A policy that affords extra cash for room and board to aid the Insured financially

72. *A Conversion Privilege is included in a Group Policy:*

........a. To enable an Insured to increase the coverage under his policy regardless of the condition of his health

SELF-QUIZ

........b. To protect the insurance company and the employer

........c. To give the Insured the right to change his coverage from a Group Policy to an Individual Policy within a certain time after leaving his job or the Group

........d. To allow an Insured to transfer his insurance coverage from one Group to another regardless of his health history

73. *Which of the following statements is correct? Malingering is:*

........a. Waiting at a hospital needlessly

........b. Prolonging a disability in order to collect more Benefits

........c. Concealing an existing disability to obtain insurance

........d. Padding a medical bill to receive greater Benefits

74. *Overinsurance exists when:*

........a. Too many people have insurance

........b. An Insured has a large amount of coverage

........c. An Insured stands to make a profit on his hospitalization or income insurance

........d. An Insured transfers his coverage from one hospital to another

75. *An insurance company may demand an autopsy under an Accident Policy in the event of:*

      I Accidental death

      II Mysterious disappearance

      III Death from natural causes

      IV A history of previous claims

The most correct answer is:

........a. I   ....c. I, III, and IV

........b. I, II, and IV   ....d. All of the above

76. *A retired person would be eligible for the following coverages:*

      I Accidental death and dismemberment

      II Medical expense coverage

      III Income coverage

      IV Hospital expense coverage

The most correct answer is:

........a. All of the above   ....c. I, II, and IV

........b. III   ....d. I and II

77. *If possible, an Insured must give Notice of Claim in:*

SELF-QUIZ

........a. 10 days   ....c. 15 days
........b. 20 days   ....d. 90 days

78. *If his insurance company does not provide a blank Proof of Loss within the required time, the Insured should:*

........a. Wait a reasonable time and make a second request
........b. Write a letter giving details of the claim and the manner in which it occurred
........c. Send a registered letter to the Agent
........d. Send a letter to the Commissioner of Insurance

79. *The insurance company must furnish a blank Proof of Loss within how many days after receipt of a Notice of Claim?*

........a. 90   ....c. 15
........b. 20   ....d. 45

80. *With respect to an Aviation Accident Policy, under which of the following circumstances would an Insured be covered? If he:*

    I Contracted pneumonia while stranded in a life boat as a result of an airplane accident (on a plane in which he was a passenger)
    II Were hurt while boarding a plane (as a passenger)
    III Were hit by a propeller (as a passenger)
    IV Were a student pilot at the time he applied for coverage and subsequently were injured in an airplane accident while learning to operate the aircraft

The most correct answer is:

........a. II, III, and IV   ....c. I, II, and III
........b. II and IV   ....d. II and III

81. *With respect to a Weekly Indemnity Policy which of the following statements is most correct? The Benefit should be:*

........a. Not more than 75% of the Insured's total income
........b. As much as the Insured can afford to purchase
........c. Enough to cover lost income and any extra expenses not otherwise compensated
........d. Not more than 75% of the Insured's earned income

82. *Proof of Loss must be furnished by the Insured to the insurance company, if reasonably possible, within:*

........a. 45 days from the date of loss
........b. 45 days from the date the blank Proof of Loss form was received

139

SELF-QUIZ

........c. 90 days from the date of loss
........d. 90 days from the receipt of the blank Proof of Loss form

83. *The Facility of Payments Clause:*
........a. Makes it easier to pay claims to the Insured
........b. Is designed to facilitate payments to hospitals and physicians
........c. Provides payment of up to $1,000 to a relative of the Insured who is apparently entitled to the money if the Beneficiary is a minor or legally incompetent
........d. Is a clause under which the insurance company may pay Death Benefits and all other accrued indemnities unpaid at the time of the Insured's death to a designated Beneficiary or to the estate of the Insured

84. *With reference to a claim, legal action may not be instituted until:*
........a. 45 days after the date the Proof of Loss was filed and not after three years from that date
........b. Evidence that the Proof of Loss was not acted upon is obtained, but not later than three years thereafter
........c. 60 days have elapsed from the date the Proof of Loss was filed and not after three years from that date
........d. Every effort has been made for a satisfactory settlement of a claim by the proper filing of a claim form and a Proof of Loss, or notification by registered mail

85. *Which of the following statements pertaining to an Industrial Health Policy are correct?*

      I Coverage is afforded for all employees working for one employer
      II Coverage is only available for employees engaged in the same industry who are members of the same union
      III Nominal Benefits are afforded for a short period of time, with Premiums usually payable weekly or monthly
      IV All of the above

........a. IV   ....c. II and III
........b. I and III   ....d. III

86. *A Commercial Health Policy affords coverage for:*
........a. Employers engaged in common commercial endeavors
........b. Employees who work only in commercial establishments

SELF-QUIZ

........c. A person who is engaged in a nonhazardous occupation; the policy contains high Benefit limits and the duration of payments is longer; the Premiums can be paid annually, semiannually, or quarterly; and the policy is cancellable

........d. A person who is engaged in a more hazardous occupation; the policy contains low Benefits which are payable for a short period; the Premiums are payable weekly, monthly, or by payroll deduction; and the policy is cancellable

87. *An Insured has a Health Policy with insurance company A affording $150 Monthly Benefits and a similar policy with insurance company B. Both policies provide for prorating with other insurers if the Insured does not notify all insurance companies concerned. The Insured becomes disabled and each insurance company discovers the existence of other insurance. How much will each insurance company pay?*

........a. A pays $75 per month and B pays $150 per month

........b. Each pays $75 per month

........c. B pays $75 per month and A pays $150 per month

........d. Each pays $100 per month

88. *A Waiver (Impairment) Endorsement is:*

........a. An agreement which waives the insurance company's liability for certain disabilities ordinarily covered in the policy resulting from a pre-existing condition

........b. A provision which exempts the Insured from payment of Premiums after he has been totally disabled for a specified period of time (e.g., 90 days)

........c. Neither an obligation of the Insured nor the insurance company; payment of Benefits and medical examinations are waived

........d. None of the foregoing

89. *All of the following statements pertaining to a Group Policy are correct except:*

........a. The insurance company must insure all eligible employees regardless of their physical condition

........b. Group Plans are Experience Rated and Excess Premiums are returned to the employer

........c. All eligible employees must receive the same Benefits

........d. Persons who do not wish to enroll in the plan for religious reasons may voluntarily waive their rights

90. *On September 10, two Health Policies that afforded protection of $49 weekly were delivered to Insureds A and B. Each had a 2-week Elimination Period and a 14-day Probationary Period. On September*

SELF-QUIZ

12, A suffered an accident which disabled him for 6 weeks. On September 19, B became ill with virus pneumonia and complications which disabled him for 5 weeks and 2 days. They would have received the following Benefits:

........a. A would get $294 and B would receive $259
........b. A would get $196 and B would receive nothing
........c. A would get nothing and B would receive $161
........d. A would get $196 and B would receive $161

91. Under the Blanket Medical Coverage portion of a Health Policy which of the following expenses are usually paid?

    I Surgeon and/or physician, registered nurse
    II Medication, braces, X-rays, and laboratory tests
    III Hospital room and board charges
    IV Blood and blood transfusions

........a. I and III   ....c. III
........b. II   ....d. All of the above

92. An Insured receives a salary of $110 a week. He has a policy with an insurance company providing for Weekly Disability Income Benefits of $25. Would you be able to write a second policy in another insurance company affording additional Weekly Disability Income Benefits?

........a. No
........b. Yes, if the total Benefits do not exceed $110 a week
........c. Yes, if the total Benefits do not exceed 80% of Earned Income
........d. Yes, if the total Benefits do not exceed 50% of Earned Income

93. An Insured may assign Benefits under his Health Policy:

    I To facilitate the making of payments directly to the hospital
    II Voluntarily to his employer, if his salary were continued
    III If his employer requested it because his salary was being paid while he was disabled
    IV To enable the insurance company to make the payments directly to his physician or surgeon

The most correct answer is:

........a. I, II, and III   ....c. I, II, and IV
........b. I, III, and IV   ....d. All of the above

94. An Agent may not share commissions with anyone except:

SELF-QUIZ

.........a. A licensed officer of another insurance company
.........b. A client who is also licensed with another insurance company
.........c. A licensed Agent of the same insurance company
.........d. None of the foregoing

95. *An Agent's license may be revoked or suspended because of:*

.........a. A violation of the Insurance Law or any law while operating as an Agent
.........b. Fraud or dishonesty, including a material misstatement in his application for a license
.........c. Incompetence or untrustworthiness while acting as an Agent
.........d. All of the above

96. *The following statements are true, except:*

.........a. An application must be made part of the policy to be admissible as evidence
.........b. A statement in an application may not be changed without the applicant's written consent
.........c. A misrepresentation in an application will always invalidate the coverage
.........d. Statements in an application are representations and not warranties

97. *Which of the following statements are correct? The Recurrent Disability Clause:*

.........a. Is a provision which states that if an Insured suffers a recurrence of his disability from the same or a related cause, the second period of disability is considered a continuation of the original disability unless the Insured has returned to work for a specified period of time
.........b. Concerns recurring Benefits if there is both a sickness and an injury disablement concurrently
.........c. Is used only for coverage of recurring illnesses
.........d. Provides for one-half or two-thirds Benefits in the event the Insured becomes disabled from the same or related causes

98. *Elective Indemnity is to a lump sum payment for a specified loss (dislocations, fractures, loss of digits) as Capital Sum is to a:*

.........a. Lump sum payment to a Beneficiary in the event of accidental death
.........b. Lump sum payment to the Insured in the event of dismemberment

SELF-QUIZ

........c. Lump sum Benefit paid for under the Double Indemnity Provision

........d. None of the foregoing

99. *A Surgical Schedule is not:*

........a. A list of Benefit allowances for various types of surgery

........b. A list showing maximum amounts payable based on the kind and the severity of the operation

........c. Applicable unless the surgery is performed in a hospital

........d. A full and complete list of all surgical procedures for which the insurance company is liable

100. *An Impaired or a Substandard Risk:*

........a. Cannot collect Double Indemnity

........b. Must submit to a medical examination in order to obtain coverage

........c. Is an applicant who is engaged in a hazardous business

........d. Is an applicant whose physical condition does not meet minimum standards for normal health

101. *John Jameson, an Agent for an insurance company not authorized to transact business in this State, sold a policy to a client. If the insurance company does not pay for a claim, which of the following statements is correct?*

........a. The State Insurance Department can enforce payment

........b. The Agent may not be held liable

........c. Claims against such an insurance company cannot be enforced

........d. None of the above

102. *Your prospect is employed full-time as a bank teller. He drives a delivery truck for his father part-time three nights each week. Under which occupation would he be rated for income protection?*

........a. As a bank teller since that is his full-time job

........b. As a bank teller, but an extra Premium would be charged for the small additional risk that his delivery job represents

........c. As a bank teller, but he would not be covered if he were injured while driving his father's delivery truck

........d. Under the classification applicable to the most hazardous job, regardless of the time actually devoted to that particular job

103. *A policyholder has a 30-day Elimination Period on his Disability Income Policy. If he becomes disabled, approximately when will he receive his first monthly income check?*

SELF-QUIZ

........a. 30 days after the start of the disability
........b. At the end of his period of disability
........c. 60 days after the start of the disability
........d. None of the above

104. *Under which of the following policies may the Insured expect to retain his protection without an increase in the Premium, regardless of the number of claims he presents?*

........a. Renewable at the option of the insurance company
........b. Guaranteed Renewable
........c. Noncancellable and Guaranteed Renewable
........d. All of the above

105. *Which of the following facts about a prospect is not necessary in order to be able to quote a Premium for an Accident Policy?*

........a. Age   ....c. Marital status
........b. Sex   ....d. Occupation

106. *All of the following clauses or provisions are mandatory under the Required Uniform Provisions Law except:*

........a. Grace Period
........b. Reinstatement
........c. Misstatement of Age
........d. Physical Examination and Autopsy

107. *Which of the following statements regarding an Elimination Period is incorrect?*

........a. An Elimination Period is the time at the beginning of a disability during which Benefits are not payable
........b. The longer the Elimination Period, the lower the Premium
........c. An Agent should always sell a policy containing a short Elimination Period so that the Insured may receive Benefits quickly
........d. An Elimination Period should be fitted to the needs of the client

108. *John filed a claim under his Disability Policy more than a month ago and still has not received a check. How long must he wait before he can bring suit against the insurance company for nonpayment?*

........a. He can bring suit at any time
........b. 3 years
........c. 60 days after a Proof of Loss has been filed
........d. He cannot bring suit to collect a claim

SELF-QUIZ

109. *Which one of the following classifications of Health Insurance is referred to in connection with Air Flight Insurance?*

........a. Commercial ....c. Industrial
........b. Limited ....d. Group

110. *All of the following are liberal clauses or provisions except:*

........a. Accidental Means
........b. Accidental Bodily Injury
........c. Nonhouse Confining Clause
........d. Nonaggregate Benefit Clause

111. *The tendency of more poor risks (than good risks) to buy and maintain their protection is known as:*

........a. Morbidity experience ....c. Mortality experience
........b. Adverse selection ....d. None of the above

112. *An Accidental Bodily Injury Clause may stipulate that loss from an injury:*

........a. Must result directly from an accident which is the unintended and unforeseeable cause of an injury
........b. Must result directly from an accident and be independent of all other causes
........c. Must result independently from any other causes by external, violent, and purely accidental means
........d. Any of the above

113. *If an Insured changes his occupation to one that is less hazardous:*

........a. Some insurance companies will accept an application for a reduction in Premium
........b. Benefits will be increased to those afforded for the Premium paid for the Insured's current occupation
........c. The policy becomes void unless the insurance company is notified within 60 days of such change
........d. None of the above

114. *An Agent is prohibited from making incomplete comparisons between Health Insurance Policies. Which of the following factors must be taken into consideration when making a comparison between such policies?*

I Gross Premiums, Dividends, and increases in Cash Values

SELF-QUIZ

   II Differences with respect to the length of time for which Premiums will be paid
   III Differences in limitations, conditions, or provisions which affect (directly or indirectly) the Benefits afforded under the policy
   IV Any other Benefits afforded under the policy

........a. II and IV
........b. I and III
........c. I, II, and III
........d. All of the above

115. *Under the Uniform Policy Provisions (in most States), the Incontestable Period for Health Insurance Policies may not be longer than how many years?*

........a. One
........b. Two
........c. Four
........d. Five

116. *A written Notice of Claim must be furnished to the insurance company within how many days after the occurrence or commencement of any loss?*

........a. 20
........b. 30
........c. 45
........d. 90

117. *If a claim form is not furnished by the insurance company within a stipulated number of days after the claimant furnished the Notice of Claim, he is deemed to have complied with the requirements of the policy with respect to the filing of a Proof of Loss if he submits a written statement describing the occurrence, the character, and the extent of the loss for which the claim is made. Within how many days must the claimant submit this statement?*

........a. 45
........b. 20
........c. 15
........d. 90

118. *Unless an insurance company had previously notified the Insured in writing of its refusal to reinstate, a policy is considered reinstated, if the insurance company doesn't communicate with the Insured beyond how many days?*

........a. 30
........b. 20
........c. 15
........d. 45

119. *Rebating is:*

........a. Convincing a friend to drop his existing Health Insurance in order to buy a policy from the insurance company you represent
........b. Good business
........c. Unethical, but not illegal
........d. Returning some of your commissions to your client; the practice is unethical and illegal

SELF-QUIZ

120. *Convincing a friend to drop his existing Health Insurance protection to purchase a policy from the insurance company you represent is:*

........a. An excellent sales idea

........b. Twisting, and is illegal

........c. In the best interest of the client because you can provide better service

........d. Unethical, but not illegal

121. *A policy which affords first dollar Benefits for hospital room and board, surgical, and medical expenses is known as:*

........a. Disability Income ....c. Hospital Expense

........b. Major Medical ....d. All of the above

122. *A policy which affords Benefits for medical expenses on a Co-insurance Basis after a Deductible is known as:*

........a. Major Medical ....c. Disability Income

........b. Hospital Expense ....d. Blanket Insurance

123. *Which of the following statements is correct? Coinsurance is:*

........a. A risk shared by several insurance companies

........b. Cost sharing by the Insured and the insurance company, usually 75%-25% or 80%-20%

........c. The amount the Insured must pay before he is eligible for Benefits

........d. All of the above

124. *The amount of expenses between the Basic Group Hospitalization Plan and the Group Major Medical Plan that the Insured must pay before he is eligible for Major Medical Benefits is known as:*

........a. Coinsurance ....c. Waiting Period

........b. Corridor Deductible ....d. Disappearing Deductible

125. *The advantage to the Insured of the Deductible and Coinsurance Provisions of a Major Medical Policy is:*

........a. Lower cost for the insurance

........b. An aid in controlling claim expenses

........c. Insurance companies are enabled to make higher Benefits available at lower costs

........d. All of the above

SELF-QUIZ

126. *A Newspaper Accident Policy is an example of which type of policy?*

........a. Commercial
........b. Limited
........c. Group
........d. Industrial

127. *Individuals engaged in any of the following occupations are insurable for Disability Income Insurance except:*

........a. A salesman
.....b. A bricklayer (seasonal)
........c. An accountant
........d. A bank teller

128. *The class of Health Policy which should be sold to a Preferred Risk is:*

........a. Limited
........b. Industrial
........c. Commercial
........d. Group

129. *Mr. Jones receives a salary of $1,000 a month. He also receives $300 a month income from investments. The amount of income that should be considered when he applies for a Disability Income Policy is:*

........a. $1,000
........b. $1,300
........c. None
........d. $300

130. *The small additional charge for the initial Premium which is sometimes paid to the Agent as part of his commission is known as a:*

........a. Service fee
........b. Loading factor
........c. Policy fee
........d. Cost of acquisition

131. *A policy which may not be terminated by an insurance company by written notice (and a refund of Unearned Premium) is known as what type of policy?*

........a. Industrial
........b. Commercial
........c. Guaranteed Renewable
........d. Limited

132. *If, after an Insured has read his policy, he decides that it is not what he desires he may return it and receive a full refund of his Premium if he does so within:*

........a. 48 hours
........b. 10 days
........c. 15 days
........d. 30 days

133. *A Substandard Risk may be underwritten by:*

........a. Charging an extra Premium
........b. Issuing an Exclusion Rider

SELF-QUIZ

........c. Issuing a policy with a longer Elimination Period
........d. All of the above

134. *An Individual Policy written on a group of persons not qualifying for true Group Insurance is known as:*

........a. Fraternal Insurance   ....c. Commercial Coverage
........b. Franchise Insurance   ....d. Industrial Benefits

135. *Insurance Laws covering twisting, rebating, and incomplete comparisons:*

........a. Are applicable to Life Insurance, but not to Health Insurance
........b. Apply to both Life and Health Insurance
........c. Protect Agents only
........d. Protect the public only

136. *Acquisition costs are included in which of the following:*

........a. Raw Premium   ....c. Short Rate Premium
........b. Pro Rata Premium   ....d. Expense Loading

137. *The charge for Interim Term Coverage is known as what type of Premium?*

........a. Earned   ....c. Fractional
........b. Short Rate   ....d. Net Cost

138. *The size of type used for printing Health Policies in most States:*

........a. Is not regulated
........b. May not be smaller than 10 point
........c. Must be larger than 20 point
........d. Is unimportant since all policies contain Standard Provisions

139. *The Principal Sum in a Disability Income Policy is the amount paid for accidental loss of:*

........a. One hand and one foot   ....c. Sight of both eyes
........b. Life   ....d. Both hands or both feet

140. *All of the following statements regarding the requirements of the Federal Fair Credit Reporting Act are true, except:*

........a. An insurance company must inform an applicant for Health Insurance (in writing) that an investigative inspection will be conducted and that the applicant is entitled to request additional information regarding the report

SELF-QUIZ

........b. Upon written request by the applicant, the insurance company must furnish information with respect to the nature and scope of the investigation

........c. The information furnished by the insurance company must contain medical information

........d. If coverage is denied or a higher rate is charged because of information contained in a report, the insurance company must inform the applicant that the denial or the increased rate resulted from the report; in which case, it must give the name of the reporting agency to the applicant

141. *An Insured secured a Health Policy containing a Change of Occupation Clause on January 1, 1973. On January 1, 1976 he changed his occupation to one which is classified by the insurance company as being less hazardous. On June 1, 1976, he notified the insurance company about his change in occupation. He is entitled to a refund as of what date?*

........a. January 1, 1976   ....c. Next Premium due date
........b. June 1, 1976   ....d. March 1, 1976

142. *If an applicant has two Disability Income Policies, the following can be assumed:*

........a. He is overinsured

........b. He is trying to defraud the insurance companies

........c. The Benefits will be prorated by the insurance companies

........d. Both insurance companies are aware of the existence of the other policy

143. *In which of the following cases may a Noncancellable and Guaranteed Renewable Health Policy be cancelled:*

    I Nonpayment of Premium

    II Within the first 60 days after the inception date of a policy provided that the insurance company gives the Insured 10 days' notice

    III At the request of the Insured

    IV At the request of the Beneficiary

Which is the most correct:

........a. I   ....c. I and III
........b. I and II   ....d. All of the above

SELF-QUIZ
ANSWERS

1. c	30. c	59. c	88. a	117. d
2. d	31. d	60. a	89. c	118. d
3. b	32. c	61. d	90. b	119. d
4. b	33. a	62. c	91. d	120. b
5. c	34. b	63. b	92. c	121. c
6. d	35. d	64. a	93. d	122. a
7. d	36. c	65. a	94. c	123. b
8. c	37. a	66. a	95. d	124. b
9. d	38. c	67. c	96. c	125. d
10. d	39. c	68. c	97. a	126. b
11. d	40. d	69. c	98. b	127. b
12. a	41. c	70. c	99. d	128. c
13. a	42. c	71. a	100. d	129. a
14. a	43. b	72. c	101. c	130. c
15. b	44. c	73. b	102. d	131. c
16. c	45. c	74. c	103. c	132. b
17. c	46. d	75. a	104. c	133. d
18. a	47. c	76. c	105. c	134. b
19. c	48. b	77. b	106. c	135. b
20. a	49. d	78. b	107. c	136. d
21. d	50. c	79. c	108. c	137. c
22. c	51. d	80. c	109. b	138. b
23. c	52. c	81. d	110. a	139. b
24. c	53. d	82. c	111. b	140. c
25. a	54. a	83. c	112. d	141. a
26. a	55. b	84. c	113. a	142. c
27. c	56. b	85. d	114. d	143. c
28. a	57. a	86. c	115. b	
29. c	58. b	87. b	116. a	